THE SEA WORLD BOOK OF
DOLPHINS

BY RANDALL R. REEVES AND
STEPHEN LEATHERWOOD

ILLUSTRATED WITH PHOTOGRAPHS

Harcourt Brace Jovanovich, Publishers
San Diego   New York   London

Requests for permission to make copies of
any part of the work should be mailed to:
Permissions, Harcourt Brace Jovanovich,
Publishers, Orlando, Florida 32887.

LIBRARY OF CONGRESS CATALOGING-IN-PUBLICATION DATA
Reeves, Randall R.
 The Sea World book of dolphins.
 Includes index.
 Summary: Describes the evolution,
physical characteristics, habits, and natural
environment of various types of dolphins.
 1. Dolphins—Juvenile literature. (1. Dolphins)
I. Leatherwood, Stephen. II. Sea World.   III. Title.
QL737.C432R44 1987 599.5'3 86-32004

ISBN 0-15-271957-1

Printed in the United States of America

 B C D E

ACKNOWLEDGMENTS

Our debt to colleagues for their
observations of dolphins is partly reflected
in the photo credits and the list of
references. There are, of course, many
others who have contributed to our
education about dolphins. In particular, we
wish to thank Bernd and Melany Würsig,
Sam H. Ridgway, Lawrence G. Barnes,
David E. Gaskin, Edward D. Asper, Randall
S. Wells, Susan Kruse, Tas'an, Kenneth S.
Norris, William F. Perrin, Chen Peixun,
William E. Evans, Lanny H. Cornell, David
K. Caldwell, and Melba C. Caldwell, all of
whom read portions of an early draft of this
manuscript to help us get the text right; of
these, many offered us unpublished insights
from their extensive experience with
dolphins. Pieter Folkens generously allowed
us to reproduce his splendid illustrations
and prepared the map and figure with the
assistance of Charlotte Carlisle. Kathy
Kangas did the typing and helped with
many other aspects of this book. We
appreciate her cheerful assistance.

"Sea World" is a registered
trademark of Sea World, Inc.

First page photograph: A Hawaiian
spinner dolphin (*M. and B. Würsig*)

Title page photograph: Bottlenose
dolphins playing in a big wave off
Maui, Hawaii (*B. Würsig*)

Dedication page photograph: A
bottlenose dolphin delights a small
boy at Sea World's Petting Pool.
(*S. Leatherwood*)

CONTENTS

To Justin

THE REMARKABLE DOLPHIN
CHAPTER ONE

Picture a herd of a thousand dolphins, dramatically and gracefully splashing and playing—clicking, squeaking, flipping, spinning, and slapping the surface of the water with their tails. Like colts kicking up their heels in a spring pasture of new grass and wildflowers, these underwater beings are apparently overjoyed at just being alive.

The sight is unforgettable, and so is the remarkable dolphin—a large-brained, sociable, creative animal whose ability to adapt to a variety of conditions rivals our own.

An animal that produces an amazing array of sounds. A sound that may be loud enough to stun or even kill the fish it

needs to eat. Or a sound too high for us to hear—as much as eight times higher than the upper limit of the human hearing range.

An animal that "sees" with its ears, using a sophisticated technique called echolocation to find its next meal, and can even assist humans in catching *our* next meal.

Picture warm-blooded creatures that do all this in the water. That breathe air, hunt, eat, play, bear their young and nurse them with milk, all without ever coming onto land.

It's easy to see why this energetic animal has fascinated everyone from Aristotle and other scholars of ancient Greece to

Dolphins nurse their young with milk. This day-old Commerson's dolphin was born at Sea World of San Diego. (*G. Reed, Sea World, Inc.*)

the creators of a popular 1960s TV show called "Flipper," which featured a lovable bottlenose dolphin always ready for adventure.

As entertaining and appealing as dolphins are, it has been difficult to learn much about them. Their lives are spent mostly underwater, which makes them hard to study. But almost every time a careful observer joins dolphins, however briefly, there are interesting and sometimes surprising things to discover.

People have long realized that dolphins are not fish. They are mammals. This means they are warm-blooded, breathe air, bear their young alive (instead of laying eggs), and nurse them with milk, just as humans do. Although most mammals have hair on their bodies, dolphins do not, except for a few bristles on the snout. Within the large group of animals called mammals, dolphins, porpoises, and whales are a subgroup, or order, called Cetacea (pronounced see-*tay*-shuh). The word Cetacea comes from the Greek word *ketos* and the Latin word *cetus*, both meaning "whale."

Fish breathe with gills, taking oxygen directly from the water, and have no reason to come to the surface for air. But

Preceding spread: Part of a large herd of Fraser's dolphins charges through warm tropical waters. (*G. Friedrichsen*)

cetaceans, though totally committed to a life in the water, must come to the surface regularly to breathe. Some occasionally beach themselves briefly while chasing food.

Are dolphins the same as porpoises? There is no easy explanation for the ways people have argued and made decisions about which is which. In our opinion, the use of "dolphin" or "porpoise" is, in most cases, a matter of personal preference. Although this book's title refers only to dolphins, the contents cover all the animals known as dolphins or porpoises.

To add to the confusion, the word "dolphin" is sometimes used to refer to a colorful oceanic fish from the tropics that is served in restaurants as mahi-mahi or *dorado*.

Besides being unlike fish and like other mammals, what is special about dolphins?

Dolphins come in many shapes, colors, and sizes. Some are fast swimmers, some slow. As a group, they are more sociable than not. Many kinds of dolphins assemble in large herds containing hundreds or even thousands of individuals. Some keep their distance, while others eagerly approach boats, zigzagging playfully in the bow wave—the wave produced as a boat moves through the water. Some like to jump and frolic; others show very little of themselves when they breathe. The antics of the more playful dolphins include aerial somersaults, body twists, back flips, and side slams.

This playfulness has captured the imagination of researchers, poets, and children of all ages. The spotted dolphin, for example, is known for its high jumps. It jumps over twenty feet above the surface for no obvious reason—except perhaps for the sheer fun of it. The spinner dolphin will jump from the water and spin along its axis, sometimes making seven or more complete turns in a single leap! The spinner dolphin reminds us of a ballet dancer or a figure skater in a high-speed pirouette.

One of the exciting things about dolphins is the way they have populated the planet. In about thirty-eight different forms—called species—they inhabit all but the coldest corners of the world's oceans. Working from the land outward, we have placed each of the dolphin species in one of four categories to show how they're distributed.

Spotted and spinner dolphins, which often travel together, are high jumpers and aerial acrobats. (*B. Würsig*)

First are the river dolphins. It may come as a surprise to you that dolphins live in some of the great rivers of the world, including the Amazon and Orinoco in South America, the Changjiang (Yangtze) in China, the Indus in Pakistan, the Ganges and Brahmaputra in India and Bangladesh, the Mahakam in Borneo, the Irrawaddy in Burma, and the Mekong in Vietnam and Cambodia. Several of the true river dolphins live their entire lives in fresh water.

The second kind, coastal dolphins, live much of their lives within a few miles of land along open coasts and inside bays, lagoons, and river mouths. Their activities often relate in some way to the tide—the daily rise and fall of water levels in response to the gravitational pull of the sun and the moon on the earth.

Third are the continental-shelf dolphins. Submerged rims called continental shelves border each of the seven continents—Europe, Asia, Africa, North and South America, Australia, Antarctica—as well as the world's larger islands. The shallow waters above these shelves are known for their productivity; most of the fish caught and consumed by people comes

Top: Clear water is something new to this mother and calf boutu, brought to the oceanarium from a muddy South American river. (*D. Caldwell*)

Center: The coastal Indo-Pacific humpbacked dolphin is at home in shallow water very near shore. (*P. Doggett*)

Left: A small band of coastal Heaviside's dolphins frolics in rough seas off southwest Africa. (*J. Gates*)

from these waters. It is no surprise to find continental-shelf dolphins thriving there, too, in great variety and numbers.

The fourth kind are oceanic dolphins, which are not as common. The high seas are not as productive as the continental shelves, and there are vast stretches of ocean where dolphins are few and far between. There are few species of these hardy dolphins, and those that do exist are not well studied.

Before taking a closer look at these four categories of dolphins, we will tell you something of what is known about how dolphins evolved and how they adapted physically to an aquatic existence. To conclude, we will illustrate what we have been able to learn from dolphins in captivity, and we'll discuss the importance of the conservation of these amazing creatures.

We are eager to share with you what we have learned about dolphins from our own work and that of our friends and colleagues. There would be little to say about dolphins if some difficult and often creative approaches to studying them had not been developed and tried.

Above: The handsome striped dolphin is widely distributed in temperate and tropical regions of the open sea. (*R. Pitman*)

Right: Common dolphins on the bow of a vessel on the broad continental shelf of western Baja California (*B. Würsig*)

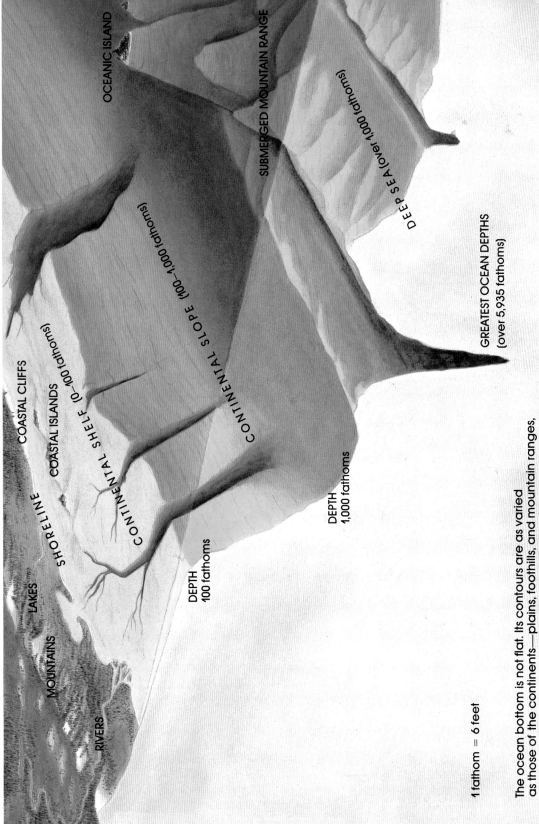

RIVERS

MOUNTAINS

LAKES

SHORELINE

COASTAL CLIFFS

COASTAL ISLANDS

CONTINENTAL SHELF

CONTINENTAL SHELF (0—100 fathoms)

CONTINENTAL SLOPE (100—1,000 fathoms)

OCEANIC ISLAND

SUBMERGED MOUNTAIN RANGE

DEEP SEA (over 1,000 fathoms)

DEPTH
100 fathoms

DEPTH
1,000 fathoms

GREATEST OCEAN DEPTHS
(over 5,935 fathoms)

1 fathom = 6 feet

The ocean bottom is not flat. Its contours are as varied
as those of the continents—plains, foothills, and mountain ranges,
with their plateaus, peaks, and valleys. (P. Folkens)

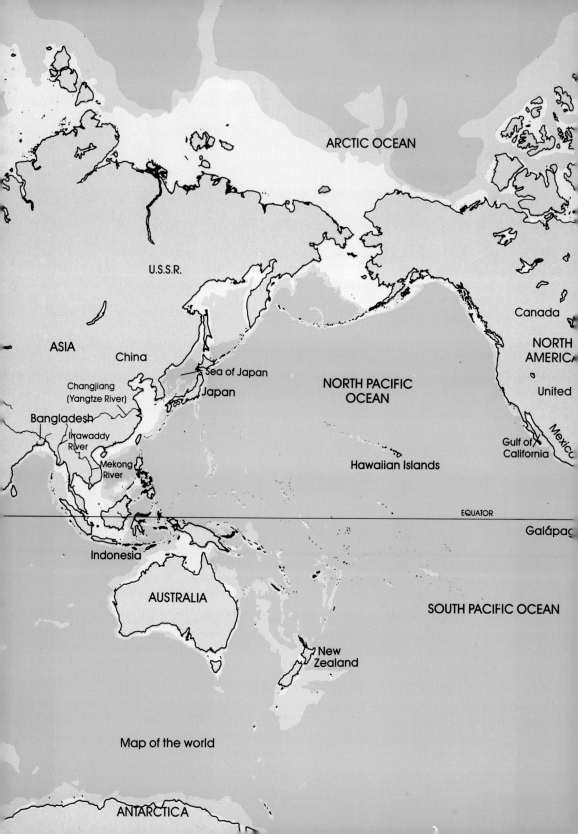

ARCTIC OCEAN

U.S.S.R.

Canada

ASIA

NORTH
AMERICA

China

Sea of Japan

Changjiang
(Yangtze River)

Japan

NORTH PACIFIC
OCEAN

United

Bangladesh

Irrawaddy
River

Gulf of
California

Mexico

Mekong
River

Hawaiian Islands

EQUATOR

Galápag

Indonesia

AUSTRALIA

SOUTH PACIFIC OCEAN

New
Zealand

Map of the world

ANTARCTICA

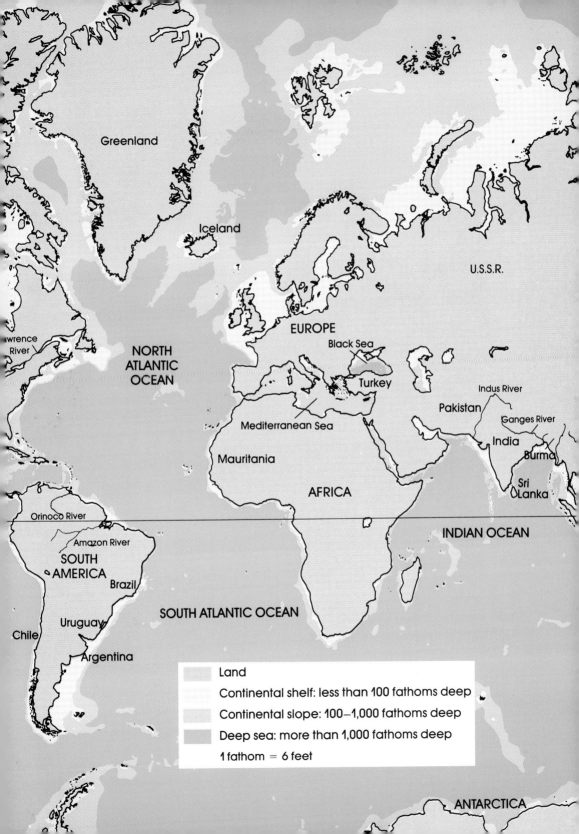

HOW
DOLPHINS EVOLVED
CHAPTER TWO

Dolphins (and all mammals, including people) are part of a comparatively recent episode in the history of life on earth. Life originated in the sea billions of years ago. Not until 500 million years ago did organisms such as snails and worms appear. In the following 100 million years, some animals crawled out of the water. Amphibians (salamanders, toads, and frogs) and reptiles (snakes, lizards, and turtles) were among the first to take up life on land. Then, during the Age of Reptiles, between 65 and 230 million years ago, some of the largest reptiles—dinosaurs—returned to the sea.

The earliest mammals appeared at least 200 million years

ago. They were small and lived in a world dominated (on land at least) by reptiles. Eventually, some mammals followed the pattern set by reptiles and returned to the sea. It was once believed that the early ancestors of whales and dolphins evolved directly from small insect-eating mammals. Now scientists think the ancestors were large flesh-eating mammals that began venturing into the water, probably to find food.

It's hard to believe, but cetaceans and hoofed mammals—such as camels, pigs, deer, and antelope—probably share some of the same early ancestors. Whales and dolphins have been evolving away from land mammals for at least 45 million years. Thousands of cetacean species have lived during these years, flourished for a time, then become extinct. They have come—and gone—in many sizes and shapes, with different ways of propelling themselves, catching food, and socializing.

The first whales, which existed long before dolphins, had torpedo-shaped bodies with short necks, paddlelike front legs, and small hind legs. Over time, their facial bones and jawbones became longer. The nose moved back between the eyes, and the nostrils ended up on top of the head. This allowed the ani-

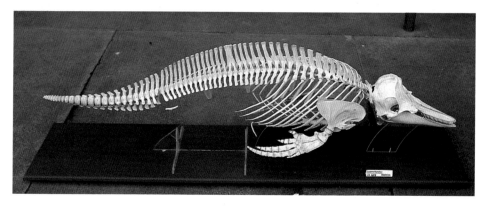

Preceding spread: Over millions of years dolphins have become beautifully adapted to life in the water. (*J. Roberts, Sea World, Inc.*)

Above: The streamlined skeleton of a dusky dolphin (*S. Leatherwood*)

Bottom: An artist's idea of what an early ancestor of dolphins may have looked like (*P. Folkens*)

mal to surface and breathe without interrupting the smooth forward motion of the body. (Imagine how much excess motion could be eliminated by human swimmers if they had no need to turn their heads when taking a breath during a race!)

The paired nostrils of land mammals became a single blowhole in dolphins. (When a dolphin breathes out, or blows air from its lungs, it is called a "blow.") An efficient plug developed to prevent water from leaking into the lungs, and also a powerful set of muscles formed to open the blowhole for breathing.

Paleontologists are scientists who study the changes over thousands or millions of years in the form, structure, and ecology of organisms such as dolphins. They search cliff faces and dried-up riverbeds for fossils, the hardened bones of long-dead animals. Often they find only pieces of an animal's body—a partial jawbone here, an ear bone there. Sometimes they find a whole skeleton or complete skull. They compare the fossils to living animals and determine what the extinct forms might have looked like and how they might have lived.

From this slow and difficult process, paleontologists have learned that the major modern groups of cetaceans appeared about fifteen million years ago. Dolphins as we know them existed about ten million years ago. We wish we could say exactly when, where, and how the distant ancestors of dolphins took up life in the sea, but these are mysteries as yet unsolved.

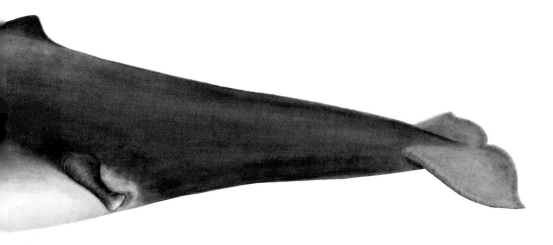

Top: Dolphins have a single blowhole located on the top of the head. (*Sea World, Inc.*)

Bottom: This rough-toothed dolphin began to blow before reaching the surface. (*R. Pitman*)

Top: Although most fossils are hard material, they are often fragile. These paleontologists have wrapped a fossil dolphin in plaster and burlap to keep it from crumbling while they excavate it. (*S. Barnes*)

Bottom: Examining skulls, two paleontologists ponder the relationship between a modern river dolphin (*foreground*) and a fossil dolphin. (*M. J. Stokes, Natural History Museum of Los Angeles County*)

HOW DOLPHINS HAVE ADAPTED
CHAPTER THREE

One challenge facing an aquatic mammal is regulating its body temperature. Anyone whose teeth chatter after a few minutes in an unheated swimming pool knows that our bodies lose heat much faster in water than in air. But dolphins have a remarkably efficient barrier against heat loss: a layer of fat, called blubber. Only the flukes, flippers, and dorsal fin lack a blanket of blubber.

In general, the closer to the equator, the warmer the water. Even within regions, however, there can be abrupt changes in water temperature caused by factors such as currents, weather, and time of day. Also, oceanic water is layered; surface temper-

atures differ from temperatures at considerable depths.

The behavior of a dolphin also varies—from traveling to feeding to resting. These activities require different amounts of energy, the most active behavior costing the most energy and thus heating the animal's body the most. So dolphins need a way to get rid of excess heat as well as insulate themselves against heat loss.

Humans eliminate excess body heat by sweating when the weather gets hot or during periods of intense activity—running, playing ball, skipping rope. Dolphins, however, have no sweat glands. They have a different way of getting rid of body heat.

As you remember, the dorsal fin, located in the middle of the dolphin's back, and the flippers and flukes lack an insulating blubber layer. All are richly supplied with blood vessels, some of which, deep in the extremities, are arranged in a special structure called a counter-current heat-exchanger.

Each heat-exchanger consists of an artery (which carries blood from the heart out to the extremities) surrounded by a circle of veins (which carry blood from the extremities back to the heart). When the dolphin needs to conserve body heat, much of the blood pumped to the appendages goes out through the artery and returns through its associated veins. Heat lost by the outgoing blood is mostly recovered by the incoming

Preceding spread: The hourglass dolphin has adapted to life in the cold Antarctic Convergence. (*F. Kasamatsu*)

Above: The tall dorsal fins of three Risso's dolphins "loafing" at the surface (*P. Howorth*)

Left: The dolphin's appendages—dorsal fin, flippers, and flukes—play an important role in heat regulation. (*S. Leatherwood*)

blood. That heat is returned to the body core rather than lost into the sea. When the dolphin needs to get rid of excess heat, its temperature and blood pressure rise, causing the arteries to bulge. This leaves less space for their associated veins, which means they carry less blood. Blood is then forced to return to the heart through veins near the body surface. The heat escaping from these veins goes mainly into the sea, and the dolphin cools down. The counter-current heat-exchange system helps keep the dolphin's body at a constant 98.6°F (37°C), the same as a normal human body temperature.

Diving presents another major challenge to a dolphin. All mammals, dolphins and humans alike, need oxygen to live. Humans can dive for only about three minutes, and to depths no greater than about one hundred feet, before having to surface for air. Scuba (self-contained underwater breathing apparatus) allows us to go deeper, for longer, but still we cannot come close to matching the diving capabilities of dolphins. Relative to their weight, dolphins have more blood than humans do, and their blood is better at binding and carrying oxygen

Tuffy, a bottlenose dolphin, assisted U.S. Navy divers in the open sea. Though unrestrained, Tuffy did not swim away from his trainers. (*U.S. Navy*)

than ours is. In addition, dolphins have a greater capacity for storing, distributing, and using oxygen within the muscles, and a greater tolerance for carbon dioxide and other by-products of respiration.

A bottlenose dolphin named Tuffy was trained in the open sea off Point Mugu, California, to dive when he heard a buzzer and to stay underwater until a second buzzer sounded. Tuffy proved to be capable of staying underwater for six minutes without difficulty even though he had used up most of the oxygen in his lungs after only three minutes. As a dolphin dives, its body makes adjustments to conserve oxygen. Its heart beats more slowly. Its blood vessels constrict, preserving blood for the heart and brain, the two organs that need it most.

Tuffy would dive to a certain depth and exhale into a funnel before surfacing. This helped scientists learn how dolphins could make repeated long dives with no ill effects. (*U.S. Navy*)

Experiments with Tuffy also showed that a bottlenose dolphin can dive comfortably and repeatedly to depths of about five hundred feet. But after diving to nearly one thousand feet, Tuffy was out of breath and had to stay at the surface for several minutes before making another dive.

Deep dives present other challenges besides the requirement for oxygen. The deeper the dive, the greater the pressure of the water on the body. You can feel this pressure on your ears when you dive to the bottom of a swimming pool. If you could swim deep enough, your chest would begin to hurt because of the pressure on your ribs, which are rigid.

Dolphins have developed ribs that are "hinged" at several places so that they can collapse or expand with variations in water pressure. Tuffy showed this when he triggered a special underwater flash camera and took his own pictures. The resulting photographs showed Tuffy's rib cage pressed out of shape anytime he was photographed below two hundred feet.

Human divers worry about getting the "bends," a painful and potentially fatal condition that occurs when a person surfaces too quickly after a long dive. Nitrogen bubbles in the

When a bottlenose dolphin dives below about 200 feet, its rib cage is distorted from water pressure. (*U.S. Navy*)

bloodstream get larger as the diver comes to the surface and may damage body tissues and become lodged in blood vessels if not reabsorbed.

When dolphins make dives deeper than three hundred feet, the high water pressure and their bodies' response to the pressure prevent significant amounts of nitrogen from going into the blood. But what happens when a dolphin makes many shallower dives rapidly, one after the other, as it might while feeding in the wild? Scientists have been able to measure the amount of nitrogen in such an animal's muscle tissue. Although the level was found to be high enough to make a human very sick, the dolphin appeared unaffected. Apparently, dolphins have special chemicals in their blood that prevent the formation of clots and bubbles. This gives them some resistance to the "bends," even after a long series of shallow dives.

Dolphins have adapted to face yet another major challenge. Visibility in the water can be obstructed by anything from mud and sand to the billions of tiny plants and animals collectively called plankton. Dolphins would live in a blind fog were it not for their ability to "see with their ears." Sound, rather than light, is a dolphin's most important source of information about its surroundings.

Sound, the vibration transmitted by a moving object to its environment, travels almost five times faster in water than in air, and dolphins have excellent hearing. They use it to listen to the sounds of fellow herd members, other animals (such as competitors, potential prey, and enemies), and the environment. Many dolphins make almost constant chirruping or whistling sounds, like those made by flocks of birds, as if to tell other dolphins: "I'm here, I'm here, I'm here." Many dolphin sounds are ultrasonic, too high for humans to hear. Dolphins produce and hear sounds as much as eight times higher than the upper limit of our hearing range.

Dolphins use sound to navigate and to locate food with a technique called echolocation or biosonar, which is the sonar (**sound navigation ranging**) used by animals such as bats and cetaceans. Sonar involves producing sounds that, upon striking an object, reflect back to the animal as echoes (thus the name "echolocation"). Dolphins can determine quickly and accurately where a sound comes from.

If you have ever heard your own echo bouncing back to you off the walls of a cave or a large empty room, then you can

Echolocation permits the dolphin to locate and catch fish even when visibility is poor. (*H. Hall*)

begin to understand how a dolphin's sonar works. Some blind people are better at echolocating than sighted people. They apparently can use echoes from the *tap-tap-tapping* of a cane to tell them where some obstacles are. But even the best human echolocators can be confused easily by too much background noise or complex echoes.

Not so with dolphins (or bats in air). Even when blindfolded, dolphins can tell the difference between tiny targets made of the same material and only slightly different in size. Dolphins can pick out their favorite kind and size of fish from a school containing many different fish.

How do dolphins traveling in groups avoid being confused by echoes bouncing off their companions? A dolphin's body absorbs much of the sound put out by other dolphins echolocating nearby, particularly at those times when dolphins are closing in on their prey. So there is little or no echo from anything except the food. This makes hunting, especially cooperative hunting, easier.

Dolphins project sound from an unusual area—just below and in front of the blowhole. It travels forward in a narrow beam, so the echolocating dolphin is like a miner finding his way through the dark with a headlamp on his hard hat.

Dolphins can produce very loud sounds. They might use some of these sounds to stun, possibly even to kill, the fish they eat. All sounds are really pressure waves that travel through water or air. Many fish have organs called lateral lines, which are especially sensitive to pressure waves. The lateral lines enable fish to move together gracefully as a school and to avoid predators whose approach is preceded by a wave, like that from a boat pushing through the water. The same sensitivity may also damage the fish, much as our hearing can be damaged by sounds that are too loud.

Cinematographer Howard Hall has filmed small fish, which had been buried in the sand, swimming upward slowly, as if stunned, or at least frightened out of their hiding places, by a dolphin's sounds. The dolphin moved along the bottom, eating the fish one at a time.

Just how smart are dolphins? This cannot be answered eas-

Some dolphins, like these northern right whale dolphins, travel in groups of ten to thousands of animals. (*R. Pitman*)

ily. There are major differences among the various species of dolphins. For example, bottlenose dolphins have much larger brains, in relation to their body size, than river dolphins. But brain size is not necessarily the only measure of intelligence. The complexity of a species' social system may be an indication of its intelligence. Some dolphins seem to form close and lasting relationships and cooperate in caring for young, finding and catching food, and protecting one another from enemies.

Are dolphins smart enough to have a language? The notion that they might be came largely from work sponsored by the government's air and space agencies. The goal was to develop ways of communicating with any intelligent life forms encountered during space explorations. Scientists recorded dolphin sounds and tried to understand what they meant to other dolphins. They also tried to establish communication between humans and dolphins.

The experiments raised many fascinating questions. But, contrary to many reports, they did not prove that dolphins have a language or that communication with them is yet possible.

Dolphins can be creative. In one experiment, rough-toothed dolphins learned they would receive a fish only when they did

A rough-toothed dolphin in Hawaii learned that only novel behavior would be rewarded. (*Sea Life Park*)

something their trainer had never seen them doing before. They proved themselves capable of satisfying this requirement and never went hungry.

Dolphins do appear to communicate minimally with one another and with other species, even humans. For example, trainers can easily tell when a dolphin in their care is feeling happy, sad, tired, or playful. The dolphin may stop performing, or it may start doing things that are not part of its usual routine. It can show excitement at seeing its trainer arrive, or pleasure at having its skin rubbed.

But such expressions of satisfaction or dissatisfaction are seen in many other animals, and we do not jump to the conclusion that they have a language or even that they are especially intelligent. For example, your pet dog can communicate to other dogs how it is feeling and what actions are required of the other dog to avoid conflict. And it can communicate to you that it is angry, happy, or hungry, or that it wants to go outside. We do not yet have proof that dolphins are capable of more than that.

Bottlenose dolphins often form close emotional bonds with their trainers. (*U.S. Navy*)

Dr. Frank Awbrey, a biologist who studies dolphin sounds and intelligence, has written: "People want so much to be able to talk to animals that they cannot believe that noisy animals are not talking to each other and even trying to talk to us. In reality, virtually all the tales of humans and dolphins communicating are self-deception. Usually, someone sees that an animal can learn to respond to spoken commands and becomes convinced not only that it understands every word it hears, but also that it is attempting to hold intelligent discourse (conversation) with humans."

Dolphins are large-brained, sociable, creative, and communicative. But how *intelligent* are they? One trouble with the question is that it too often means simply: "How much are they like people?" When asked that way, the question becomes easier to answer. Dolphins and other wild animals have been shaped by millions of years of evolution to meet the challenges of their own environment. They represent nature's best attempt, so far, to fill a particular role in the natural world. Dolphins are not, however much we may wish they were, "little people in wetsuits." They are perfectly equipped to survive in a liquid environment inhospitable to most other mammals. And that is enough.

RIVER DOLPHINS
CHAPTER FOUR

There are no modern river dolphins in North America, Europe, or Africa. They live only in Asia and South America. One species, the **baiji** (BAY-gee), lives only in the Changjiang (formerly the Yangtze River) in China. Two species, the **boutu** (BOH-too) and the **tucuxi** (too-koo-SHEE), inhabit the vast Amazon and Orinoco river systems of South America.

Although they share much of the same habitat, boutus and tucuxis differ in many ways. The strange-looking boutus have been described as "beady-eyed, humpbacked, long-snouted, loose-skinned holdovers from the past." They look as though they belong in a world populated by dinosaurs and other long-

extinct life forms. They move slowly and sluggishly, often surfacing without the rapid, rolling movement characteristic of most dolphins. Some people refer to the boutu as the pink dolphin. The source of the pinkish cast, particularly seen in older individuals, is probably the blood vessels very near the surface of the skin. Coloration seems to be related not only to age but also to the clarity of the water the dolphin lives in. Boutus tend to darken when placed in the clear water of an aquarium tank.

Tucuxis have a more streamlined appearance than boutus. They move quickly and roll smoothly at the surface. Unlike boutus, which are often found alone or in pairs, tucuxis are usually seen in groups of two to five animals. Boutus live only in fresh water, while tucuxis inhabit coastal saltwater areas as well.

Boutus and tucuxis become inhabitants of the jungle or rain forest during at least part of the year. In October and November, the driest months in the great Andes mountain range, the rivers draining these mountains reach their lowest levels. To survive, dolphins, the Amazon manatee, and even fish must stay in the

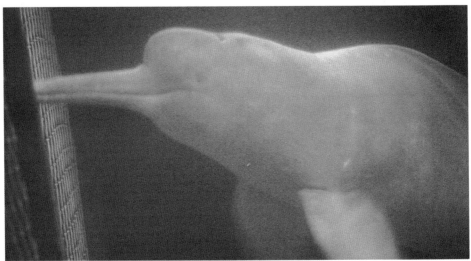

Preceding spread: A tucuxi swims alongside a fishing canoe in Brazil. (*W. Hoek*)

Top: The baiji lives only in China's Changjiang, where its survival is threatened by pollution, boat traffic, and entanglement in fishing gear. (*M. Nishiwaki*)

Bottom: The boutu has been called "the ugly dolphin."

main river channels and the deeper lakes. During the wet season, water levels rise dramatically, and the jungle is flooded. Lakes that were entirely cut off during the dry season once again connect with an endlessly twisting network of waterways. Rivers that were mere trickles become fast-flowing avenues of muddy water, carrying branches, tree trunks, and clumps of vegetation toward the sea. Dolphins, especially boutus, venture far from the rivers and onto the jungle floor during this season.

This annual cycle of flooding and drying-up creates special problems—and opportunities—for the dolphins. Obviously, they need to remain in water deep enough for swimming. But they also need to find enough food, avoid predators, and maintain a certain amount of social contact with one another. It is especially important that they give birth to their young when conditions are just right for survival.

In the Amazon at least, both boutus and tucuxis wait until the dry season to give birth. Fish are forced to congregate in the deep channels, and the dolphins have an easier time finding food. This makes it a good time for calving. Mothers can keep themselves well nourished while providing milk to their rapidly growing newborn calves (baby dolphins). By the time heavy rains start again, the calves are big and strong enough to accompany their mothers in the search for fish outside the main river channels and on the flooded jungle floor.

The two species have quite different diets. Tucuxis eat small schooling fish that live in relatively deep water, while boutus prefer fish that live alone on the bottom of rivers and lakes. The tucuxi's teeth are cone-shaped, like those of most marine dolphins. The boutu has a special set of teeth at the rear of its jaws. These are wrinkled and rough, rather than pointed. After a boutu catches a fish near the tip of its jaws, it moves the fish toward the back of its mouth, where it crushes or chews it before swallowing. No other dolphin has crushing teeth like these, which are similar to our own molars.

One researcher has seen giant river otters feeding close to a riverbank, with a group of dolphins feeding a few yards farther out from the bank. He guessed that the dolphins were catching fish that were fleeing toward deeper water to escape from the otters. He wondered if the dolphins were listening for the characteristic alarm call of the otters—a "HAH!" snort—to help them avoid predators. Twice the otters noticed the researcher and gave their openmouthed "HAH!", and the nearby dolphins responded with several sharp, noisy blows of their own and jumped partially out of the water.

Top: Two Amazonian boutus in the Brazilian jungle. The lead animal's long snout and bulbous head are visible to the right. (*W. Hoek*)

Left: A tucuxi leaps with a fish held crosswise in its mouth. (*D. Magor*)

Right: A curious Irrawaddy dolphin eyes the diver/photographer. (*S. Leatherwood*)

You may have noticed the same kind of cooperation among different wild creatures. Jays, mockingbirds, and other feathered sentries of the forest often are the first to detect an intruder. Their alarm calls can send squirrels, deer, and other animals scurrying for cover. This simple form of communication between species provides useful security for all.

The murkiness of the Amazon, Orinoco, and their tributaries, especially when water levels are high, makes vision of limited use to a river dolphin. The boutu's snout has many bristles that allow the dolphin to probe in the muddy bottom with its snout, "feeling" for prey. Although boutus have tiny eyes and a well-developed echolocation capability, they apparently can see well.

Certainly they can see better than their distant cousins that live in the Indus, Ganges, Brahmaputra, Meghna, and Karnaphuli river systems of the Indian subcontinent. The **susus** (SOO-sooz), as these dolphins are known, have no crystalline lens and are virtually blind. Probably the most they can tell about their environment is how bright or dark it is.

Unlike the boutu and tucuxi, the Indus susu knows no jungle or rain forest. The land bordering the Indus River is a desert, with less than ten inches of rain each year; in the driest years major sections of river may be cut off to the dolphins by dried-up shallows. The Ganges susu inhabits some of the most polluted waters on earth, in the Hooghly River near Calcutta, India. It also lives in the treacherous Sundarbans, the vast, swampy lowland at the mouth of the Ganges River noted for its man-eating tigers, and in various rivers in mountainous, landlocked Nepal.

The susu is a plump dolphin. While being transported, for example, boutus are flexible enough to turn around in a box only twenty-three inches wide, while susus of a similar weight are simply too fat to turn around in the box. Young susus have a long, narrow beak armed with wicked-looking inch-long teeth. In older animals the teeth become flattened, sometimes worn down all the way to the gum line.

Unlike any other dolphin whose swimming style has been observed, the susu normally swims on its side. While most dolphins use their flippers mainly for steering, these blind river dolphins feel along the bottom with one of theirs, much as we humans might use our hands to feel our way through a darkened room. As the susu swims, its head moves constantly, scanning the bottom with its sonar clicks.

Susus are almost never silent, and almost never still. We suppose their constant sound production means that they are processing echolocation signals almost continuously. Their continuous motion may be necessary to prevent the dolphins from being swept away by the sometimes powerful currents of the river.

Other dolphins besides the tucuxi live both in rivers and along coasts. Many scientists believe that the **Irrawaddy dolphin**, named for the Irrawaddy River in Burma, is more closely related to the beluga or white whale of Arctic seas than it is to other river dolphins. Not as restricted in distribution as the name

Left: The remarkable spitting behavior of the pesut is apparently used to herd fish. (*S. Leatherwood*)

Right: The finless porpoise inhabits coastal waters, bays, and rivers in the Indo-Pacific region. (*W. J. Houck*)

suggests, Irrawaddy dolphins are found in warm, tropical waters throughout much of the northeast Indian and southwest Pacific oceans. They seem to prefer coastal areas, particularly the muddy, brackish waters at river mouths, but they also travel far up some large rivers. In Indonesia, these dolphins are called **pesut** (peh-SOOT).

In certain rivers (the Irrawaddy in Burma, the Mekong in Cambodia, and the Mahakam and its tributaries in southeast Kalimantan, Borneo) the pesut appears to migrate. During periods of moderately high water, it pursues fish far up the rivers. It moves back to the deltas and adjacent coasts during dry periods between monsoons (heavy rains), when river water levels are lowest, and during peak flooding.

In Kalimantan, where rain forests are rapidly being cut down, the Mahakam and Pela rivers are cluttered by boat traffic and choked with logs, debris, and silt from logging operations. One small population of pesut (about a hundred animals) no longer migrates downstream seasonally as it once did. The logging pollution has probably had an effect on the fish migrations in these rivers and, in turn, on the dolphins' food supply.

Collectors from the Jaya Ancol Oceanarium captured sixteen members of the Pela River population and flew them by helicopter to Djakarta. Twelve were still alive in 1986, and two had given birth to healthy calves.

Both the wild dolphins in Kalimantan and the captives at the aquarium use an amazing method for herding and encircling fish in shallow water. Two or more dolphins swim roughly side by side, driving a school of fish in front of them. Periodically, the dolphins spit mouthfuls of water ahead of themselves and alongside the school of fish. This scares the fish and keeps them in line with the advancing dolphins, which eventually manage to catch and eat them.

Those dolphins in the aquarium's pools may soon be all that remains of the Pela River population. We can only hope that the people who see the dolphins performing there will take a greater interest in what is happening to the world's rivers and forests.

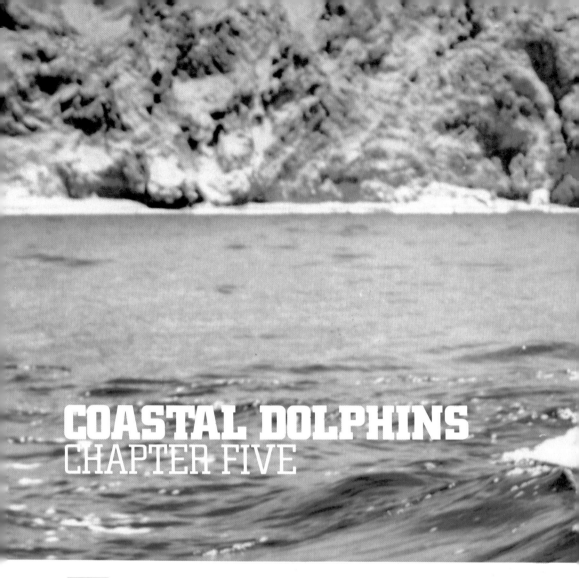

COASTAL DOLPHINS
CHAPTER FIVE

The distribution of coastal dolphins is defined by the borders of continents, as well as the coasts of some islands. In many places coastal dolphins can be seen from land. Most of them are used to seeing and hearing humans and are familiar with boats and fishing gear.

Not much is known about some coastal dolphins, such as the **franciscana**, or **La Plata dolphin**. Though closely related to the river dolphins, the franciscana lives an entirely marine existence in coastal waters of Uruguay, Brazil, and northern Argentina. It has a long beak lined with nearly 250 teeth, more than in any other mammal.

But another coastal dolphin, the **bottlenose dolphin**, is unquestionably the most familiar and thoroughly studied dolphin in the world. It was a bottlenose dolphin that starred in the long-running television program "Flipper," and this species is the one most often seen performing in dolphin shows. It can adapt to a variety of conditions, from the high seas to a local marina. It eats just about anything that swims or wiggles in the water (except fellow mammals): shrimp, worms, squid, crabs, and fish of many kinds.

Shrimp nets make bottlenose dolphins' lives simple along the Gulf of Mexico coasts. They follow the working shrimp boats,

Preceding spread: Bottlenose dolphins near the eastern shore of Isla Angel de la Guardia, Baja California. (*R. Storro-Patterson*)

Above: Coastal bottlenose dolphins can be good surfers. (*W. Perrin*)

Left: A fisherman carries a franciscana caught in a gill net along the coast of Uruguay. (*R. L. Brownell*)

devouring fish, shrimp, and other morsels that fall out of the nets or are stirred up as the nets drag through the bottom mud. When the catch is being sorted, they eat the unsalable or "trash" fish that the fishermen throw over the side.

Dolphins congregate where passes have been dredged to connect the open sea with salty, sun-baked lagoons, moving in and out of the ship channels looking for food. In marshes along the coast of South Carolina, bottlenose dolphins chase schools of mullet into the shallows. After driving the fish onto the beach, the dolphins follow, wriggling across the mud flats to snatch up their flapping prey.

Bottlenose dolphins near Saratosa, Florida, sometimes use a "fish-whacking" technique. During summer months, the dolphins chase fish in water less than four feet deep. When they overtake the fish, they whack them with a powerful swing of their flukes. The fish fly as far as thirty feet through the air and land helpless on the surface.

Bottlenose dolphins often swim with whales. Off California in winter, they accompany herds of pilot whales following spawning squid and gray whales that come close to the coast as they migrate. Researchers in Florida occasionally get reports of right

Bottlenose dolphins in the Gulf of Mexico often approach shrimp boats to eat discarded "trash fish." (*S. Leatherwood*)

whales being "attacked" by "sharks." When they investigate, it invariably turns out that the whale was being mobbed by a group of bottlenose dolphins.

We do not know why bottlenose dolphins and some other small cetaceans mob whales this way, as small songbirds might mob a hawk or crow. Small birds have an obvious reason for making the lives of large birds as miserable as possible: they are defending their nests and nestlings. But dolphins have nothing to fear from the whales they mob. Perhaps they pester their huge distant relatives just for the fun of it.

Different approaches have been tried for studying bottlenose dolphins. For example, most dolphins have nicks or scars on their dorsal fins. Using photographs of these well-marked fins, scientists can identify, and reidentify, week after week, year after year, individual wild dolphins. With a good camera and plenty of film, many mysteries about these animals' lives can be solved.

How long they live can be estimated by removing one of the dolphin's approximately ninety teeth. Like the trunk of a tree, where annual growth rings provide a permanent record of the tree's age, the tooth of a dolphin, once cut in half, can be read to determine how old the dolphin is. In this way scientists have found that some bottlenose dolphins may live forty years or more.

The society of wild bottlenose dolphins appears to be fairly well organized. Mothers with calves of a similar age tend to swim together, as do females unaccompanied by calves. Many of these females may be closely related to one another. Adult males roam alone or in groups of two or three, frequently visiting but not joining the female groups. The bonds between adult males may be formed early in life and can remain strong over many years.

Large bands of juvenile dolphins consist mainly of males that have left their mothers' female group. It may be that, like teen-aged humans, these juvenile dolphins seek the security and adventure of associating with companions their own age. The females in these bands will eventually become attached to a group of adult females. The males, which mature later in life than the females, may finally decide on a buddy or two. Even-

Researchers have come to know many of the bottlenose dolphins off Sarasota, Florida, like "Killer," shown here with her calf. (*R. Wells*)

tually the males split away from the group, in pairs or trios, or sometimes alone.

For a number of years Sea World of Florida, in cooperation with the University of Miami and Hubbs Marine Research Center, has been studying bottlenose dolphins in an approximately one-hundred-mile stretch of the Indian and Banana rivers along the east coast of Florida near Cape Canaveral. Several hundred bottlenose dolphins are year-round residents of this lagoon network. Scientists have been able to trace the animals' movements, evaluate their associations with one another, and estimate their rates of growth. Individual dolphins tend to stay in the same area and to remain a part of the same group for years, though they do have some contact with herds in distant parts of the lagoon system and even in the Atlantic Ocean.

Research is not the only reason for dolphins and people getting together. Since ancient times there have been stories about coastal dolphins behaving in a friendly manner toward people. For example, the Imragen—fishing people who live on the edge of Africa's Sahara Desert—rely on a good winter's catch of mullet to see them through each year. In years when the mullet do not appear or the catches are low, the Imragen may face considerable hardships, even starvation. But when one of the huge migrating schools of mullet is running close along the coast, the Imragen have been known to catch more than two tons of fish within half an hour. They do it with the help of dolphins!

Early in the morning, fishermen sitting on the beach can spot a passing mullet school by the slight change it causes in the color of the water. One of them walks into the water and begins violently beating the sea with a stick. He keeps up a rhythm of one stroke every four to six seconds for a few minutes. Soon dolphins appear on the horizon, racing toward the beach.

An Imragen fisherman and a coastal dolphin trapping a school of mullet
(R. G. Busnel)

The fishermen, working in pairs, carry their nets on their shoulders as they wade into the water. When they are up to their armpits, they begin to surround the mullet with the nets. The scene becomes one of wild excitement, with panicking mullet jumping several feet in the air. The dolphins swim rapidly among the fish, between the nets, and even around the fishermen's legs. Then, suddenly, peace is restored. The mullet that have escaped the nets and the dolphins' jaws continue their coastwise migration. The dolphins return to deeper water. And the fishermen draw ashore their heavy nets, bulging with fish.

Two kinds of dolphin participate in the Imragen's fishing parties—bottlenose dolphins and **Atlantic humpbacked dolphins**, which have a peculiarly shaped dorsal fin. It is as though the fin itself is on a thick platform rising to make a "hump" in the middle of the back. Humpbacked dolphins have a more restricted distribution than bottlenose dolphins, which are found throughout much of the world. They live along the west and east coasts of Africa, the continental borders of the Indian Ocean, the coasts of Australia, and the coast of eastern Asia as far north as China.

The Indo-Pacific humpbacked dolphin usually can be recognized by the thickened base of its dorsal fin. (*T. Palagyi*)

Coastal dolphins have been helping mullet fishermen make their catch in this way in West Africa and elsewhere for some time. Aborigines living on offshore islands in Moreton Bay, eastern Australia, used to catch mullet and tailor (a late-winter schooling fish) with the assistance of dolphins. Cooperative mullet fishing may have also taken place in the Mediterranean Sea during ancient times. Pliny the Elder wrote almost two thousand years ago of people catching mullet with the aid of dolphins along the coast of what is now southern France.

In Shark Bay, on the west coast of Australia, a group of bottlenose dolphins has become friendly with people in another way. Over the past twenty years, local fishermen and tourists have come to recognize about thirteen individual dolphins. The dolphins are given colorful names like Crooked Fin, Holey Fin, Old Speckledy Belly.

Every day at least several of the dolphins appear, eager to interact with children and others who wade into the shallows. A local dog, Ringer, counts on a daily romp with the dolphins, waiting patiently for them to appear. He swims up and down the beach with them, or heads out into deeper water for a game of hide and seek, the dolphins diving out of sight while Ringer paddles and searches for his playmates. The dolphins allow people to pet them and even accept dead fish that the people offer by hand.

Most similar instances of wild bottlenose dolphins becoming friendly with people have involved lone dolphins. What is remarkable about Shark Bay is that so many members of a local herd numbering more than fifty animals choose to interrupt their daily routine to play with humans.

A smaller, more businesslike coastal cetacean is the **harbor porpoise**. It measures no longer than about six feet and weighs up to two hundred pounds. It lives in the cooler waters of the Northern Hemisphere—along the Asian, American, and European coasts, around Greenland, Iceland, and the Faroe Islands, and on some offshore banks such as the Georges and Grand banks in the western North Atlantic.

As small animals living in a cold environment, harbor porpoises cannot be lazy in their relentless search for food. If they

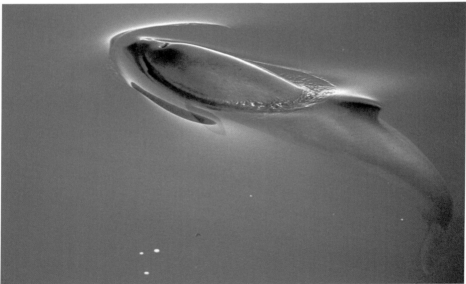

Top: The wild bottlenose dolphins of Shark Bay, Australia, enjoy the companionship of children and pets. (*E. Gawain*)

Bottom: An exceptionally clear look at a harbor porpoise. Normally, these animals are shy and avoid boats. (*D. Butcher*)

are to maintain a sufficiently thick blubber layer to insulate them against water as cold as 35°F (about 2°C) and at the same time keep some fat in reserve for times when food is scarce, harbor porpoises must keep busy.

Unlike many of the playful dolphins that gladly take time off to bow-ride or perform acrobatic leaps into the air, harbor porpoises usually roll at the surface quickly and smoothly, with no wasted motion. The explosive *puff* as they blow out and *suck* as they breathe in has earned them the nickname "puffing pigs."

Harbor porpoises may live no longer than about thirteen years and do not reach maturity until three to five years of age. Normally, a female harbor porpoise in her prime, living in an environment where food is plentiful and easy to catch, may produce one calf each year for several successive years—no more than about four, possibly as few as two or three, calves in the course of her lifetime. At this rate, every young harbor

This harbor porpoise trapped in a herring weir off the coast of New Brunswick, Canada, was released unharmed. (*R. Olsen*)

porpoise becomes a valuable investment for the population's survival.

The harbor porpoise has three near relatives with restricted distributions: the **spectacled porpoise** of southeastern South America, the **Burmeister's porpoise** of southern and western South America, and the **vaquita** (pronounced vah-KEY-tah) of northwestern Mexico.

South of the equator live four other species of small coastal cetaceans: **Hector's dolphin** around New Zealand, the **Chilean dolphin** off southwestern South America, **Commerson's**

Heaviside's dolphins live only along the southwest coast of Africa, usually in water shallower than 500 feet. (*J. Gates*)

dolphin off eastern Argentina and Chile and around the Falkland and Kerguelen islands, and **Heaviside's dolphin** off southern and southwestern Africa. Most have been little studied. In many areas these dolphins have an unfortunate habit of getting tangled in fishing nets, and some are harpooned for use as crab bait. Because all four species have such restricted distribution, they could be endangered by unregulated catching.

These dolphins, the largest of which are scarcely five-and-a-half feet long and 150 pounds, are all beautifully colored in shades of charcoal and tan on a background of stark white. We know some can swim relatively fast. In one recent encounter, six Heaviside's dolphins came to a ship's bow and stayed with it for over an hour as it steamed down the coast at about ten miles per hour. Small bands of dolphins also rode the bow waves of inflatable boats launched from the ship. The dolphins had no trouble overtaking and keeping up with the boats while the outboard motors were at full throttle.

Just how fast can dolphins swim? The question is very difficult to answer. People who see them at sea say that dolphins can catch up and stay with a boat traveling twenty-five miles per hour or faster.

But it's impossible to tell if the dolphins are approaching from an angle, or from directly behind the vessel. If you have seen a film showing lionesses attacking zebras, you've noticed how important the angle of attack is. A lioness has no chance of catching up to a zebra in a simple footrace. But if she can sneak up from the side without being noticed, then begin the chase at a favorable angle, she can claim the advantage. Dolphins may overtake some boats the same way.

We can say with complete confidence that some dolphins swim at speeds as fast as twenty miles per hour. The Dall's porpoise, considered one of the fastest small cetaceans, can overtake a boat traveling twenty miles per hour, ride in its bow wave for a few minutes, then speed up and swim ahead of the boat for a short distance before veering off to the side.

A Pacific white-sided dolphin can overtake a boat traveling no faster than about sixteen miles per hour. It can stay in the bow wave if the boat's speed increases to twenty miles per hour, but as soon as it leaves the bow wave it veers off to the side and falls behind the boat.

In the northern Strait of Magellan (near the southern tip of South America), the currents flow at speeds of at least sixteen miles per hour as they pass at high tide through two narrows, each less than a mile across. At times of day when boats with powerful engines avoid the narrows, Commerson's dolphins move there at will, somehow managing to keep from being swept away or left stranded high and dry. It's a truly impressive sight to see them swimming, at home in the cold, swirling water of the strait.

The high-speed Dall's porpoise creates a "rooster tail" of spray as it streaks along the surface. (*S. Leatherwood*)

DOLPHINS OF THE CONTINENTAL SHELF
CHAPTER SIX

The coastal dolphins just discussed are inhabitants of the continental shelf, which begins at the shoreline and continues seaward until the water is one hundred fathoms (six hundred feet) deep. But there are other species of dolphin inhabiting the shelf that do not come close to the coast as regularly as the coastal dolphins. These we call continental-shelf dolphins.

Dusky dolphins, along with their close relatives—**Peale's dolphins, Atlantic and Pacific white-sided dolphins**, and **white-beaked dolphins**—are good examples of continental-shelf animals. Dusky dolphins off the Patagonian coast of Argen-

tina move across much of the shelf in small groups, usually containing between six and fifteen individuals. Twenty to thirty
small groups, totaling up to four hundred animals, are often
seen. Dusky dolphins off southern Peru, northern Chile, and eastern New Zealand have been seen in even larger groups, some
containing nearly a thousand dolphins.

　　The daily rhythm of the dusky dolphins of Argentina is based
on the behavior of the southern anchovy, a small schooling fish
less than four inches long. During the day, anchovies travel in
dense schools; at night they spread out. Dolphins find fish like
anchovies easier to catch when they are packed close together.

A herd of dusky dolphins moves close to shore, perhaps in search of prey. (*S. Leatherwood*)

So during summer days dusky dolphins hunt; at night they slow down and rest. In winter the dolphins seem to rest more during the day and to make deep dives at night. This must mean that acceptable food is not near the surface in winter. (Dolphins, like other animals, will not go out of their way to work harder for a meal than is necessary.)

A feeding herd of dusky dolphins can usually be seen at some distance because of the birds that are attracted to the area. The dolphins chase a school of fish toward the surface, making them easy pickings for the terns and gulls wheeling overhead. After presenting the birds with an almost-free lunch, what do the dolphins get in return?

As a herd of dusky dolphins spreads out in search of food, the small groups can get out of hearing range of one another. But somehow the message that food has been found reaches groups of dolphins as far as five miles away from the feeding site. Such groups have been seen hurrying along a straight course toward the fish school. As they do, some members of the group leap high out of the water. The dolphins' high leaps would be like a periscope raised from a submarine—a way of getting above the water surface for a clear look at the horizon.

Preceding spread: A tight group of racing common dolphins (*R. Wells*)

The closer they get to the goal, the lower these leaps become. Perhaps it is the flock of hungry birds that tells the distant dolphins where to go. After a while, the dolphins can proceed without any more high leaping, instead homing in on the sounds of a meal in progress.

The high leaps by dusky dolphins might serve other purposes. They may confuse or frighten the fish and keep them in a tight school. Also, they may alert other dolphins that dinner is on the table, so to speak.

A more acrobatic type of leaping takes place when the dusky dolphins are finished feeding. They spin, somersault, and flip high in the air. At such times, they also play with sea lions, elephant seals, right whales, boats, and kelp. The dolphins may be doing nothing more than "kicking up their heels"—leaping and twisting simply because it feels good. This behavior may also serve to develop and strengthen friendships or other rela tionships among individuals within the herd, just as play does in humans.

In some ways, dusky dolphins are every bit as "coastal" as bottlenose dolphins. During summer at least, the dusky dolphins in Argentina spend much of the night and early morning hours in shallow water near shore. The dolphins may be putting them-

Terns wheeling above dusky dolphins suggest that feeding is in progress below the surface. (*S. Leatherwood*)

selves out of the reach of predators. A number of times when dusky dolphins have been seen in water less than three feet deep, killer whales were in the vicinity.

Not all dolphins of the continental shelf are seen in such shallow water. **Common dolphins**, for example, though they share much of the range of dusky dolphins and their kin, are more likely to remain farther offshore.

Opposite page: After a meal, dusky dolphins become playful and acrobatic. (*S. Leatherwood*)

Top: Naturalists get a close look at a white-beaked dolphin, a North Atlantic relative of the dusky dolphin. (*R. Sears*)

Bottom: The Pacific white-sided dolphin, found only north of the Equator, closely resembles the dusky dolphin of the Southern Hemisphere. (*W. Flerx*)

Common dolphins are so named because they are indeed common in cool temperate waters around the world. Their large herds, sometimes containing well over a thousand animals, attract attention with no problem. Common dolphins often approach boats to ride in the bow and stern waves, where they play and splash energetically. This appealing species has been mentioned often in literature for three thousand years.

Studies of common dolphins on the southern California continental shelf show that they generally avoid areas where the sea bottom is flat. Instead, they assemble in areas where the bottom has many slopes and ridges, which are good places to catch fish. As the currents flowing onto these rough areas move upward, they sweep nutrients off the bottom and carry them high into the water. There they nourish plants, which in turn become food for animals inhabiting the surface layers. Areas

The common dolphin has colorful markings and a lively spirit. (*S. Sinclair*)

supplied with large amounts of nutrients in this manner attract and support a great variety of life. Dolphins travel quickly from one feeding ground to another, perhaps locating the grounds by listening for the noise created by large concentrations of sea life.

The dolphins have a typical daily pattern. Near midday they assemble into large herds, apparently resting. They are not likely to ride the bow waves of boats at such times. In the early afternoon, the dolphins bunch tightly together and begin to move, with lots of jumping and splashing. In the evening, just as the sun is setting, the herd separates into many smaller groups. These groups begin to dive, exploring the depths for food.

The "deep scattering layer" is a mass of animals that is widely spread out from medium to great depths during daylight. The layer moves upward at night, and the air-breathing dolphins can then get to it with the least amount of energy. In the morning, the sun rises and the layer spreads out again and moves deeper. The dolphin groups, which have hunted independently during the night, form large herds and move toward the next night's feeding areas. Near noon they slow down again and rest.

The coastal form of the spotted dolphin is more heavily spotted than the offshore varieties. (*R. Pitman*)

Like common dolphins, both spotted dolphins and spinner dolphins come close to shore near certain islands. Near the Bahamas in the western Atlantic, teams of observers spent several summers diving with a group of about sixty spotted dolphins. They got to know some of the dolphins as individuals. One in particular, called Didi because she frequently made a sound like "di-di," became friendly with the divers. Didi seemed always to be accompanied by a remora, or sucker fish, which attached itself to different parts of her body. It is not unusual for remoras to be seen "hitching" free rides on the skin of dolphins.

Remoras keep a tight grip on a dolphin even when it jumps high in the air and comes crashing down on the very spots where the fish are attached. Sometimes remoras swim around a slow-moving dolphin and take up various positions on that dolphin or one of its companions. Remoras appear to profit from their association with dolphins by getting free rides and maybe even free lunches. How the dolphins might take advantage of their clingy associates is not so clear.

Right: A member of a herd of spinner dolphins that returns to Kealakekua Bay, Hawaii, in the early morning hours—full of noise and splash—after a night of feeding offshore. (B. Würsig)

Opposite page: Wherever they are found, the tropical spinner dolphins are willing bow-riders. (J. M. Rose)

OCEANIC DOLPHINS
CHAPTER SEVEN

Few dolphins are truly oceanic. Many of those found in deep water depend in some way on the continental shelf or on other productive areas such as seamounts (submerged islands that do not quite break the water's surface) and major ocean current systems.

A problem in studying dolphins on the high seas is the great expense of getting there and staying long enough to make useful observations. Until a few years ago, little was known about oceanic dolphins, but the American tuna fishing fleet changed all that. Publicity about the large number of dolphins killed in the course of fishing operations forced the tuna industry to carry

official observers to the fishing grounds in the eastern tropical Pacific. While developing ways to reduce the number of dolphins killed in the fishery, scientists collected information about the numbers and types of dolphins present on the fishing grounds. Just as important, they noted where no dolphins were seen.

Spinner dolphins in various parts of the tropical Pacific differ in appearance. Those in the east are almost uniformly gray. The offshore spinners have a prominent white belly, with light gray sides and a somewhat darker back. Hawaiian spinners have a white belly and a very dark back, which contrast sharply with the light gray sides and tail region. Male eastern spinners have a dorsal fin that looks as though it is on backward, and they have a peculiar bulge on the underside just ahead of the flukes. These features make male eastern spinners easy to recognize when they are swimming in a mixed herd with **spotted dolphins**. This could be of particular use to female spinners looking for a mate of their own species.

Eastern spinner and spotted dolphins have an interesting relationship. The eastern tropical Pacific is especially suited to

Preceding spread: Rough-toothed dolphins "skimming" (*R. Pitman*)

Top: Spinner dolphins off the south coast of India (*A. Alling, World Wildlife Fund*)

Right: Eastern spinners are battleship gray. (*M. Webber*)

the mixed herds of spinners and spotters and the complex of tuna and other animals with which they associate. Beneath a thin upper layer of warm water is a thick, cold layer with very little oxygen. To the dolphins, this cold layer may function like the seafloor does closer to shore. In this wide-open environment, far from any shoreline, the oceanic spinners have come to regard herds of spotted dolphins as substitutes for islands or coasts. Just as a child may depend on a teddy bear or a "security blanket," the spinner dolphins may take comfort in always knowing where they are in relation to the larger and more powerfully built spotted dolphins.

This would be a problem if the two species competed for the same food supply, but they dive and feed differently. Spinners generally dive deeper than spotted dolphins. Whatever the details of their compromise, the two species have obviously evolved a successful arrangement. It releases them both from the need to live within a short distance of a shore of some kind, and it helps make them *oceanic* dolphins.

A mixed group of spotters (*top*) and spinners (*middle and bottom*)
(*G. Friedrichsen*)

Spotted dolphins in the eastern tropical Pacific sometimes travel more than ninety miles a day, with a roughly circular home range of a two hundred to three hundred nautical-mile diameter. The placement of this home range tends to be nearer the coast in fall and winter, shifting offshore in late spring and summer.

The **clymene** (cly-MEE-nee) **dolphin**, a short-snouted spinner dolphin, appears to live only in the tropical Atlantic Ocean. Only a handful of scientists have seen and reliably identified this dolphin at sea. Several sightings were far offshore, about halfway between South America and Africa. Based on what has been found in the stomachs of several dead clymene dolphins, they eat lantern fish and squid.

Of all the dolphins, one of the most widespread and ocean-going is **Risso's dolphin**, sometimes called the grampus. It is a large dolphin, up to thirteen feet long. In addition to its tall dorsal fin and long, pointed flippers, two aspects of the grampus's appearance are especially odd. First, its head looks as though it has been given a solid, vertical, head-on karate chop. The wedgelike crease on the front of this dolphin's head is unique;

The unmistakable creased
head of a Risso's dolphin
(*S. Leatherwood*)

no other cetacean has anything like it. Second, young Risso's dolphins are largely dark brown or black, but adults eventually become almost white except for the flippers, dorsal fin, and flukes, which remain dark. Its body looks as if someone has spilled a bucket of white paint on it. It is literally plastered with white scratches and scars. Many of these are probably made by the sharp beaks of squid, which are these dolphins' favorite food; others by the teeth of their companions. Risso's dolphins have few teeth; some animals, particularly older individuals, have no teeth at all. Nevertheless, Risso's dolphins manage to catch plenty of squid.

No one has been able to make a sustained study of the behavior of wild Risso's dolphins. We know their moods vary widely. At times, they travel in loosely formed lines abreast, probably looking for food or heading for known feeding grounds. At other times, they are loafing. Such periods of rest will often end suddenly, and the dolphins will become playful and inquisitive, slapping the water, sticking their heads above the surface, jumping almost clear of the water and falling on their sides with a splash.

Though they do not usually bow-ride, one famous Risso's dolphin, nicknamed Pelorus Jack, used to greet steamships and ride their bow waves as they passed across the outside of Pelorus Sound in Cook Strait, New Zealand. He was beloved by Cook Strait mariners and residents. At least one attempt was made to kill him before a special order was issued in 1904 to protect him from being shot or harpooned. Pelorus Jack disappeared in 1912, after almost twenty-five years as a familiar and welcome friend.

The **rough-toothed dolphin** looks like a bizarre, unfinished clay sculpture of a long-nosed bottlenose dolphin. An art teacher asking students to design a "normal" dolphin would give no more than an average grade for a sculpture resembling a rough-toothed dolphin. Its flippers look large and ungainly. Its dorsal fin and the ridge along the back near its base seem to be set too high. Its eyes appear too big. Bulges in the "cheek" area give the impression of a narrow collar around the neck, separating the head from the chunky body. Most of all, the

Rough-toothed dolphins seem always to be watching their human observers. (*R. Pitman*)

head seems wrong. It is long and cone-shaped, with no sign of the crease between the beak and the rest of the face that appears in most other dolphins. Its teeth are shaped like no other dolphin's. They are wrinkled and rough, not smooth.

But, like all other modern dolphins, the rough-toothed dolphin has evolved to take advantage of a particular niche or place in the food web. It roams tropical seas in tight bands of a few to a few hundred individuals, but is not very abundant anywhere.

When they have been watched closely, wild rough-toothed dolphins have done some interesting things. For example, tightly packed groups sometimes swim at high speed, their chins and beaks skimming along the surface like the front tips of water skis. No one has even ventured a guess as to why they swim this way.

A rough-toothed dolphin was once photographed in a group of ten individuals swimming through the clear blue waters off Hawaii. In its jaws was a twenty-pound mahi-mahi, or dolphin fish, of which the other dolphins partook. Were the dolphins sharing willingly, like lionesses that have cooperated to make a kill, or was the owner being robbed of its dinner by its herd-mates? No one knows.

As well as in the eastern tropical Pacific, small dolphins live far from any coast in one of the roughest stretches of ocean in the world—the Antarctic Convergence. Between the continent of Antarctica and the southern coasts of Africa, South America, New Zealand, and Australia, there are no large land masses to interrupt the almost constant gales and the roll of wind-driven seas. Strong currents, usually flowing from west to east, help form a sharp boundary between polar waters, influenced by the icy waters and chill winds of Antarctica, and the cool temperate waters farther north.

The high productivity of the Antarctic Convergence, with its abundance of plankton and fish, explains its appeal to the two species of dolphin that live in and near it. The **hourglass dolphin** and **southern right whale dolphin** are probably able to

From their markings, it is easy to see how hourglass dolphins got their name. (*J. Gates*)

make their living in the featureless expanses of open sea only because of the special conditions created by the Antarctic Convergence.

Hourglass dolphins are named for the shape of the large white patches on their sides. They are energetic dolphins often seen in small bands charging through the water with a flock of seabirds dipping overhead. When not busy with some impor-

A bow-riding southern right whale dolphin (*F. Kasamatsu*)

tant activity of their own, hourglass dolphins are enthusiastic bow-riders, a welcome sight in the cold and often rough waters where they live.

There are two species of right whale dolphin, a northern one that lives only in the North Pacific and a southern one that lives near the Antarctic Convergence. Right whale dolphins are so named because, like right whales but *unlike* almost all other dolphins, they lack a dorsal fin entirely.

Right whale dolphins do not seem to miss the absent fin. They can swim very fast, at least twenty miles per hour, and change direction as quickly as other dolphins. Their markings are striking, and the border between black and white zones is sharp. Herman Melville (a sometime whaler, but better known as author of the classic novel *Moby Dick*) called the southern right whale dolphin the "mealy-mouthed porpoise" because it looks as if it has just dipped its nose in a sack of white flour.

Fraser's dolphins have a dark stripe along the side. (*R. Pitman*)

CAPTIVE DOLPHINS
CHAPTER EIGHT

The keeping of wild animals in captivity, in some cases leading to domestication, is nearly as old as human history. Humans began keeping dogs (closely related to wolves and coyotes) and cats (related to lions and leopards) as pets and eventually learned to control their reproduction and establish the various "breeds." The same is true of cattle, horses, sheep, goats, even chickens and ducks. These familiar farm animals are all the results of ancient efforts to domesticate wild animals and turn them into companions, helpers, and sources of food for people.

Sea mammals have never been domesticated, though

some early steps have been taken in that direction. For example, a few sea lions and harbor seals have been kept alive for years in small swimming pools and treated for all intents and purposes like pets. Manatees and dugongs, large plant-eating aquatic mammals, have often been kept alive by fisherfolk, either in backyard pools or tied to ropes to restrain them in canals, lagoons, or other waterways. The animals are fed grasses and other plants to keep them alive until they are needed, often for special occasions that call for a feast.

Manatees have also been brought into semi-captivity and used as aquatic lawn mowers. Scientists once hoped that by putting large numbers of manatees to work clearing the fast-reproducing water hyacinth from canals and reservoirs, they could insure the survival of dwindling manatee populations in Florida and Central and South America. As far as we know, this idea has not been put into practice on a large enough scale to see if it would work.

More than a hundred years ago, the first aquariums were built in Europe, England, and North America. Boston's Aquarial Gardens had, by the early 1860s, obtained a white whale (beluga) and a porpoise. Few cetaceans, other than white whales taken from the St. Lawrence River in Canada, were brought into captivity until the early 1900s. Marineland of Florida became the first permanent dolphinarium in the 1930s. During the last fifty years or so, dolphins and small whales have become popular as display animals and performers.

Our knowledge about how to insure the animals' comfort and good health in controlled environments has also grown. The first white whales and bottlenose dolphins were transported in wooden shipping crates, with moist seaweed placed in the

Above: At Duisburg Zoo, Germany, a beluga from Canada holds a hurdle for two Commerson's dolphins from Argentina. (*S. Leatherwood*)

Preceding spread: Three Pacific white-sided dolphins seem to soar above their pool. (*J. Roberts, Sea World, Inc.*)

bottom. To protect them from overheating and their skin from drying out, buckets of water were poured over them from time to time.

Modern oceanariums take every precaution with the dolphins in their care. During capture, a team of swimmers tends netted animals while they are still in the water to keep them from injuring themselves on the net or on the sides of the boat. Swimmers and boat crews transfer the dolphins into padded slings or stretchers equipped with lined holes for flippers and special protection for eyes. They then lift the animals carefully aboard the vessel. On deck, they place them on foam pads or in U-shaped frames that support the stretchers, to distribute their weight evenly. This prevents damage to their internal organs, allows the dolphins to breathe freely, and makes it possible for their blood to flow smoothly.

In the water, a dolphin is essentially weightless. The buoyancy of the water gives it equal support over the entire body. The bones are not arranged to support the animal's full weight. So, if stretchers were not used, the dolphin would tire of lifting its own weight with each breath, much as you might tire if you were pinned under a playmate in a wrestling match and were trying to escape.

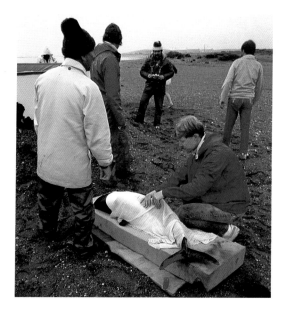

A newly captured Commerson's dolphin is placed on a foam pad and covered with a damp sheet until it can be transferred to a holding pool. (*S. Leatherwood*)

Out of water, a dolphin must also be kept moist. Otherwise, its skin will dry, and the animal will overheat. The early dolphin collectors had the right idea. But now, rather than just pouring water over the animal, attendants traveling with the dolphin often coat its exposed parts with lanolin or other moisturizing creams. They also cover the dolphin with a blanket of terry cloth or other absorbent material, being careful to avoid obstructing the blowhole. They keep this cover wet, using buckets or sprayers.

As long as these basic needs are met, dolphins can remain out of water for several days and travel long distances without harm. For example, collectors have flown river dolphins from Pakistan to San Francisco, Commerson's dolphins from southern South America to San Diego and Germany, and bottlenose dolphins from the southeastern United States to many parts of the world. A few years ago, a United States oceanarium gave some bottlenose dolphins to Jaya Ancol Oceanarium in Djakarta, Indonesia. The dolphins flew aboard a commercial jet and arrived safely at their destination after thirty-six hours of travel—a tiring ordeal for any human. For a dolphin, adapted to life in the water, it was a remarkable feat of endurance.

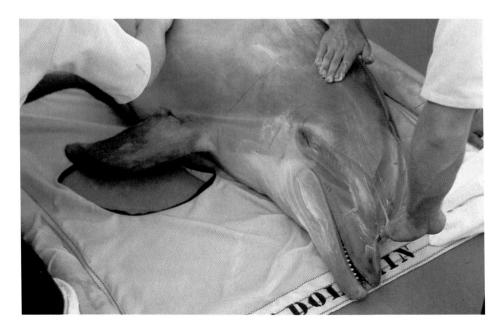

Opposite page and above: Modern oceanariums have developed safe, reliable techniques for handling and transporting dolphins. (*Sea World, Inc.*)

Sea World, building on the combined experience of the United States Navy and other organizations, has developed efficient procedures for transporting cetaceans. Moving the animals from one park to another has become almost routine. Every year, in spring, they ship dolphins, seals, and even killer and false killer whales from one park to another. In fall, the animals are returned to their winter holding sites. Special sophisticated transporters are equipped with wheels, forklift slots, and lifting lines for easy handling. They have buckles and straps to tie creatures down in airplanes and on trucks, reservoirs and filters to provide clean water, regulators for the timing of sprays and the temperature of water, and air conditioners. Highly trained attendants go along to look after the dolphins' every need. Dolphins today travel as first-class passengers.

The bottlenose dolphin has become the most familiar member of the captive dolphin community for a number of reasons. First, it is abundant along the coasts of the southern United States. Second, it is easy to capture compared to most other dolphins. Third, it readily adapts to the confinement of an oceanarium pool. After all, its natural home is in shallow water, and most coastal bottlenose dolphins have had close contact with people from a very young age. So the adjustments to noise, handling, and shallow, enclosed conditions are probably not as difficult to make as they would be for dolphins that inhabit offshore waters, where contact with people is less frequent.

Oceanariums have played an important part in teaching people to appreciate and cherish the wonders of the natural world. Many began with the main purpose of providing entertainment. But as more and more people had the opportunity to see a dazzling array of marine creatures—from sharks and rays to manatees and dolphins—the potential educational value of marine parks and oceanariums began to be realized. There is probably no better example than the experience with the killer whale.

Killer whales are the largest members of the dolphin family. (They are called whales only because of their large size.) Males grow to a length of nearly thirty feet and have a dorsal fin that can be six feet tall. Females reach lengths of about twenty-five feet. Both are handsomely marked in black and white. Both have a mouth filled with large pointed teeth.

Killer whales hunt in packs, eating whatever they want, from small fishes to fellow marine mammals, including the great whales. Even the blue whale, the largest animal on earth, is not safe from a pod of marauding killer whales. The sight of killer whales attacking a large whale probably gave them the name "whale killer," later reversed to "killer whale." It also led to misconceptions about the potential danger killer whales pose to human beings.

As recently as the mid-1960s, killer whales were widely regarded as ferocious, dangerous beasts. In 1965, a killer whale was captured alive and kept in a penned enclosure in British Columbia, Canada. It did not attack and kill its handlers. Instead, it developed a close and friendly bond with one of them, Ted Griffin. Namu, as the whale was named, allowed Ted to swim with him and ride on his back.

Since then, live killer whales, most of them caught in Washington State, British Columbia, and Iceland, have been on display at marine zoological parks in Japan, China, Australia, South America, Canada, and Europe, as well as the United

Keeping dolphins healthy and happy in an oceanarium depends on a good relationship between the animals and their trainers. (*J. Roberts, Sea World, Inc.*)

States. They have won the admiration of the public with their combination of awesome power and gentle tolerance of humans. They have learned quickly how to perform. They have impressed trainers with their personalities, which can range from playful to moody. Observations of captive killer whales have led to new thoughts about the intelligence of cetaceans. Our experience with killer whales in captivity has dramatically changed our attitudes and feelings toward them.

The crowd, the trainer, and a lucky guest enjoy a tender moment with a killer whale. (*J. Roberts, Sea World, Inc.*)

In September, 1985, a killer whale at Sea World of Florida gave birth to a healthy calf. The calf doubled its weight twice in less than a year. Its steady progress and disarming antics have been widely publicized. This birth emphasizes the direction marine zoological parks have defined for their future. More than forty bottlenose dolphins have been born at Sea World parks alone since 1978. Others have been born at other parks. In addition, some of the less frequently captured species, such as the Irrawaddy dolphin and Commerson's dolphin, have given birth to healthy young.

Like modern zoos, marine zoological parks have come to appreciate that their future depends on the development of successful captive breeding programs. The day may not be far off when there will no longer be a need to make expensive and controversial capture expeditions for bottlenose dolphins and killer whales. The marine parks will supply their own needs from a self-sustaining population of captive animals. In addition, captive breeding of endangered dolphins such as the baiji may contribute to the survival of species.

Workers from Duisburg Zoo catch Commerson's dolphins with a hoop net from the bow of their vessel off southern Chile. (*S. Leatherwood*)

Birth of an Irrawaddy dolphin: labor (*opposite page, top*); the instant before birth (*opposite page, bottom*); the calf being nudged toward the surface (*top*); its first breath (*bottom*) (*Tas'an*)

CONSERVATION OF DOLPHINS
CHAPTER NINE

As human populations grow, so do our needs for space, food, and other resources. By-products of our activities also increase, and pollution results when we do not properly recycle or dispose of them. In many cases, we compete with other animals for food—for example, by catching fish that dolphins might otherwise eat.

In the early 1950s, many people from developed nations became concerned that people in less developed countries were going hungry. The United Nations Food and Agriculture Organization, as part of its "Freedom from Hunger Campaign," tried to improve fishing methods in some coastal states. As a

model for this program, they chose Sri Lanka (formerly known as Ceylon), a small island off the southeast coast of India, in the northern Indian Ocean. Traditional fishing boats, formerly powered by paddles or sails, were equipped with motors. Brand-new boats of modern design were introduced, in some cases replacing the native craft. The traditional lines and nets of many fishermen were replaced with gill nets made of strong synthetic fibers, mostly nylon. Gill nets are large panels of netting hung vertically in the water. The way the twine is tied to make the nets leaves many openings, called mesh. Fish can swim partway through the mesh but are snagged by their fins or gills when they try to back out. These new synthetic gill nets are light, durable, and excellent at catching the fish the fishermen seek. But they are also good at catching many other animals, among them dolphins and small whales.

For many of the fishermen, there were cultural taboos against eating dolphin meat. Others simply did not know if it was good or safe to eat. They soon learned, however, that dolphin meat could be eaten or sold for profit. Gradually, local markets developed. Agents began to collect dolphins from the fish landing sites, load them into ice trucks, and transport them to villages away from the seashore. People learned to expect dolphin meat in the marketplace. Some fishermen depended on it as part or all of their income. The sale of dolphin meat became a part of the economy of the country. When the fishermen did not catch dolphins accidentally in their nets, they began to go to sea to kill them with harpoons. On a calm day, a handful of boats working together can catch over a hundred dolphins in this way. This current situation, involving extensive

Previous spread: Modern tuna seiners are responsible for the deaths of tens of thousands of dolphins each year. (*S. Leatherwood*)

Left: The worldwide spread of gill nets made of synthetic fiber poses a serious threat to dolphins, seabirds, and other marine creatures. (*S. Leatherwood*)

Right: Wherever they are used, gill nets catch more than the fish for which they are intended. Dolphins, such as these in Sri Lanka, are among the victims. (*S. Leatherwood*)

killing of dolphins off Sri Lanka, developed from well-intentioned attempts by outsiders to help the Sri Lankans feed themselves.

Scientists estimate that 15,000, or perhaps even as many as 40,000, dolphins of over a dozen different species may die each year in Sri Lankan net fisheries. Another 8,000 to 10,000 may be harpooned for use as food or fish bait. At the urging of outsiders concerned about dolphin conservation, the Sri Lankan government is now trying to convince fishermen to protect dolphins rather than kill them. But the fishermen, particularly in poorer areas, will not be won over easily.

To most of us, 50,000 dolphins sounds like an enormous number. But if there are enough dolphins in the rich waters around Sri Lanka to support some level of harvesting, who are we to demand that people stop exploiting the animals? If they stop, who will repay the fishermen, fish buyers, and shopkeepers for their loss of income? What food will replace dolphin meat in the diet of Sri Lankans? These questions are not easy to answer. But they must be considered by anyone seriously concerned about the long-term coexistence of dolphins and people, not only in Sri Lanka but in many other developing countries with growing human populations.

No matter how strongly we may oppose the killing of dol-

A dead spotted dolphin headed for the local fish market to be sold (*S. Leatherwood*)

Left: In parts of Sri Lanka where large numbers of dolphins are caught they have become significant to the local economy, which makes them harder to protect. (*S. Leatherwood*)

Below left: A fisherman with a dolphin harpoon (*R. Hahn*)
Below right: Part of a day's catch (*R. Hahn*)

phins, situations where people hunt them for food demand our reluctant acceptance. Everyone needs to eat to survive. However, there are situations in which very large numbers of dolphins have been killed, and continue to die, for no good purpose. We will give two alarming examples.

For many years, tuna fishermen have used dolphins to help them locate schools of tuna in the Pacific Ocean off Mexico and Central America. Dolphins and tuna travel together. Since the dolphins are larger and make more of a commotion on the surface, they can be spotted at greater distances than can the tuna. Feeding herds often attract birds that can be seen at even greater distances. Before the late 1950s, most American tuna fishermen caught their tuna with hook and line and sometimes ended up fishing in the middle of a herd of dolphins. Then the tuna fleet adopted new equipment that allowed the fishermen to catch more fish in less time by purse-seining them.

A tuna purse seine is a huge net, up to three-quarters of a mile long and six hundred feet deep. Once the school of tuna is

A tuna purse seine, set around fish and dolphins, is being hauled back on board. (*W. Evans*)

A large group of spinner dolphins crowds one end of a closed tuna net, waiting for an opportunity to escape. (*W. High, National Marine Fisheries Service*)

encircled, the end of the net is taken back aboard the boat. The bottom part of the net sinks. It is then drawn shut by pulling the line, much like a purse is closed by pulling the purse string. The valuable tuna are caught inside. But so are the dolphins.

Though tuna fishermen make efforts to free the dolphins before bringing the tuna on board, several *million* dolphins have been killed in the tropical Pacific tuna fishery in the twenty-five years since purse-seining began. Apart from a few thousand that have been collected for museums, no practical use has been made of these dead dolphins. They have simply been removed from the nets and thrown overboard.

The tuna fishermen mean the dolphins no harm. They have helped find better ways of getting the animals out of the nets and back into the sea alive. But tuna fishing is big business, and no one seems ready to return to the old hook-and-line method just for the sake of the dolphins.

A second example of large-scale unintentional killing of dolphins comes from Japan. A large fleet of Japanese boats fishes for salmon, using nets that are about six yards deep and 15,000 yards—nearly nine miles—long. They form a curtain of

A Dall's porpoise wrapped in a salmon gill net (*W. Everett*)

death for sea creatures that swim into them. Not only salmon, but other fish, dolphins, porpoises, whales, diving seabirds, and seals become entangled and die. Millions of birds and many tens of thousands of porpoises, particularly Dall's porpoises, have died in Japanese salmon drift nets over the past twenty-five years. Just as in the tuna fishery, their deaths have benefited no one. The carcasses either fall out of the net or are removed and thrown overboard by the fishermen. The dolphins might be sold for food in Japan, where dolphin meat is eaten. But the limited freezer space on the boats is saved for the more valuable salmon. The fishermen would rather catch only salmon in their nets, but the most efficient nets for catching salmon are also very good at catching other things. The fishermen are unwilling to give up their profits, even if it means the environment must pay a high cost.

We have seen how dolphins assist fishermen in a number of ways, but there are also times and places where dolphins hinder fishermen.

On the Kona coast of Hawaii, fishermen who catch pink snappers are sometimes dismayed to pull in merely the heads

Left: In some parts of the world, dolphins are seen as a valuable food source. Here, rough-toothed dolphins are butchered at a Japanese fish market. (*M. White*)

Right: Dolphins slaughtered at Iki Island by fishermen who saw them as competitors (*H. Hall*)

of the snappers. They know that the bodies of the fish have been torn away by dolphins. Other fishermen in the same area sometimes have to quit fishing with bait, resorting instead to artificial lures because the bait is stolen off the hooks by dolphins.

The problem supposedly began in Hawaii in about 1950 when a single wily bottlenose dolphin began stealing bait off hooks. Today, numerous dolphins, including not just bottlenoses but also some rough-toothed dolphins, have learned how to take large bait fish off hooks without getting so much as a scratch themselves. Fishermen describe the cat-and-mouse games they play with dolphins. If a dolphin has been spotted nearby, a fisherman might pull his bait in close to the boat and wait for the dolphin to leave. But the dolphin can stay underwater for so long that the fisherman is fooled into thinking it has gone away. When he lets out some line again, the dolphin promptly grabs the bait.

Understandably, the fishermen are upset. At present, no solution to this problem is in sight. Since shooting dolphins is not allowed in Hawaiian waters, there is nothing the fishermen can do without breaking the law, except stop fishing. Several methods have been tried to discourage the dolphins. Pieces of wire or extra hooks planted inside the bait are readily detected and avoided, thanks to the dolphins' sonar. Firecrackers and other noisemaking devices work briefly, but the dolphins quickly learn they are harmless. As populations of dolphins increase under legal protection and fish resources decline because of increasing human usage and pollution, such instances of competition or "thieving" can be expected to increase.

In Japan, dolphins are not protected. In most years, thousands of them—mainly striped, spotted, and bottlenose dolphins—are driven ashore to be sold in fish markets as food. Thousands of Dall's porpoises are harpooned each year from aboard coastal fishing boats in northern Japan, also for commercial sale of the meat. But even in Japan, there is a serious problem of dolphin competition with humans.

Off Iki Island in the southern Sea of Japan, fishermen spread tons of anchovies over the fishing grounds to attract the valuable yellowtail. During the late 1970s, the fishermen began to

In Alaska, a Sea World research program seeks to understand the killer whales' family relationships and seasonal movements, relying principally on the reidentification of photographed individuals. (*S. Leatherwood*)

complain that dolphins and small whales were eating the bait, stealing hooked fish, and in the process damaging their gear. Fishermen broadcasted killer whale sounds underwater and used speedboats to drive the small cetaceans away. But neither measure worked for long, and in 1977 the fishermen began driving the dolphins ashore and slaughtering them. More than a thousand animals, mainly bottlenose dolphins and false killer whales, have been killed at Iki Island.

Fishermen's retaliation is not limited to nations like Japan which view whales and dolphins principally as resources to be harvested. Recently, Alaskan fishermen reported that killer whales were stealing black cod from their lines and damaging their fishing gear. Some fishermen, in anger, started shooting at the whales. Scientists began to notice bullet wounds or scars on some of the animals they had been watching and photographing for a number of years. Some of the photo-identified whales disappeared from their pods (as family groups of killer whales are called) and were feared dead. Fishermen continue their harassment, playing loud noises and setting off explosives near the whales. So far, though, nothing has worked to the fishermen's satisfaction.

In the Black Sea, sandwiched between Turkey, Bulgaria, Rumania, and the Soviet Union, small cetaceans have been hunted commercially for just over a century. In some years the dolphin hunters have taken more than 100,000 dolphins and porpoises, and have shot and killed or badly wounded thousands more. Concerned about the effects of heavy hunting on dolphin stocks, Rumania, Bulgaria, and the Soviet Union ended their participation in the hunt in 1967. However, Turkish fishermen continued their dolphin hunt until very recently. Both Turkey and the Soviet Union are expanding their anchovy fisheries in the eastern Black Sea. Since Black Sea dolphins are believed to depend on these anchovies for food, the end of hunting is probably not the end of trouble for them.

Clearly, the problems of conserving dolphins can take many different forms. As we see it, the problems requiring the most urgent attention involve species with very limited distributions. Thus, certain river dolphins are probably the most endangered.

For centuries, the boutu enjoyed a special status among the people of the Amazon and Orinoco basins. Various superstitions have protected the species. For example, some natives believed that burning dolphin oil in a lamp caused people using the lamp to become blind. Settlers now moving into the once-impenetrable rain forests of South America have no use for old beliefs. As a result, the boutu is less and less safe from human hunters. Commercial fishermen in Brazil and Peru consider the boutu a competitor and destroyer of fishing gear; many of them shoot boutus on sight. The dolphins die when accidentally caught in gill nets. Some also become trapped in shallow pools during the dry season, cut off from the main channels because settlers dam the tributaries for irrigation. A new market has developed in Brazil for dried eyeballs and sexual organs of boutus, which are thought to make the men and women who possess them more attractive to members of the opposite sex. People buy them as charms from street vendors and even purchase them by mail order.

A young Brazilian looks over a catch of boutus along the bank of the Brazilian Amazon. (*R. Best*)

The susus in the Indus River system now number only several hundred individuals. Their once-extensive habitat has been drastically reduced and modified by the construction of dams. These dams make more water available to irrigate crops and to produce hydroelectric power, with less water available for the susus. Now divided by the dams into several separate populations, the surviving susus must depend more than ever before on the willingness of local Pakistani people to tolerate and protect them and their habitat.

The baiji is also very close to extinction. Like the susu, it lives in a water system vital to the well-being of millions of people. The Changjiang could be described as the lifeblood of China—the main artery flowing from the country's heart. Ten percent of the whole world's human population lives along its banks. For thousands of years, the Chinese have used it to water crops, to move them and their produce from the midlands toward the sea, to dispose of waste, and to produce an abundant supply of fish. The Chinese took for granted that baiji would always be a part of this great river's life, but they were alarmed recently to discover how few baiji were left. Though the several hundred survivors are strictly protected, threats from industrial development are growing as the Chinese push to modernize their economy. For instance, vessel traffic in the Changjiang is said to have doubled since 1969. Baiji get caught and drown when they try to remove sturgeon from fishermen's hooks. As their commitment to saving the giant panda from extinction has demonstrated, the Chinese are prepared to devote considerable resources to the protection of their country's wildlife. The baiji's future rests entirely in their hands.

Another cetacean with a bleak future is the vaquita, sometimes known as the cochito, a small porpoise in the upper portion of the Gulf of California (the Sea of Cortez). It was described by scientists less than thirty years ago, though of course local Mexican fishermen always knew it was there. By the time its existence became widely known outside Mexico, the vaquita was probably already in trouble. Damming of the Colorado River, a major source of nutrients for the upper Gulf of California, had already begun to damage the very limited area where these porpoises live. The totoaba, a tasty sea bass, was at that time being heavily fished with gill nets. Like its relatives, the vaquita seems unable to detect and avoid nets, and fishermen sometimes found drowned vaquitas in their gill nets. During the early 1970s, because of concern that these fish might be in danger of extinction, the totoaba fishery was officially closed by Mexico. This reduced the pressure on the vaquita as well. By 1985, however, experimental fishing for totoabas had resumed, and it was not long before more dead vaquitas were being brought ashore.

Scientists and conservationists believe the vaquita's population may be dangerously low. But because of this porpoise's small size and the low profile it presents while surfacing to breathe, it has been impossible for scientists to make a useful count. Those who have gone to the gulf and searched for vaquitas have usually returned with little more than vague descriptions of what might have been a vaquita or two. Research continues with a sense of urgency, and scientists hope to learn enough about the vaquita's behavior, movement, and biology to give it meaningful protection before this little porpoise slips into extinction.

Left: Heroic attempts are sometimes made to keep stranded dolphins alive and comfortable. Efforts to return them to the sea or maintain them in an oceanarium are usually futile. (*S. Leatherwood*)

Following page: Two vaquitas surface in the upper Gulf of California. (© *G. Silber*)

It would be wrong to leave you with the impression that all dolphins are endangered. Several species survive in large, healthy populations of many thousand, and in some cases several million, individuals. Countries such as the United States, Australia, and South Africa have passed laws protecting dolphins. People in countries like India, Burma, and Mauritania have special feelings for dolphins that make them willing to protect the animals regardless of what the law may be.

Just as we humans have proven our ability to destroy the environment and eliminate other species, we have shown that we can reverse those processes. Sea otters and elephant seals, once nearly extinct, have responded to protection by increasing their numbers. As species, they now appear to be out of danger. No success stories like these can yet be told about endangered dolphins. But there is no reason why the remarkable dolphin, given a clean and healthy environment, cannot live in harmony with the other animals, including humans, that share its world.

DOLPHINS AND PORPOISES

Common Name	Scientific Name
Rough-toothed dolphin	*Steno bredanensis*
Tucuxi	*Sotalia fluviatilis*
Indo-Pacific humpbacked dolphin	*Sousa chinensis*
Atlantic humpbacked dolphin	*Sousa teuszii*
Irrawaddy dolphin	*Orcaella brevirostris*
Melon-headed whale	*Peponocephala electra*
Pygmy killer whale	*Feresa attenuata*
White-beaked dolphin	*Lagenorhynchus albirostris*
Atlantic white-sided dolphin	*Lagenorhynchus acutus*
Dusky dolphin	*Lagenorhynchus obscurus*
Hourglass dolphin	*Lagenorhynchus cruciger*
Peale's dolphin	*Lagenorhynchus australis*
Pacific white-sided dolphin	*Lagenorhynchus obliquidens*
Fraser's dolphin	*Lagenodelphis hosei*
Bottlenose dolphin	*Tursiops truncatus*
Risso's dolphin	*Grampus griseus*
Spinner dolphin	*Stenella longirostris*
Clymene dolphin	*Stenella clymene*
Striped dolphin	*Stenella coeruleoalba*
Pan tropical spotted dolphin	*Stenella attenuata*
Atlantic spotted dolphin	*Stenella frontalis*
Common dolphin	*Delphinus delphis*
Southern right whale dolphin	*Lissodelphis peronii*
Northern right whale dolphin	*Lissodelphis borealis*
Heaviside's dolphin	*Cephalorhynchus heavisidii*
Black (Chilean) dolphin	*Cephalorhynchus eutropia*
Hector's dolphin	*Cephalorhynchus hectori*
Commerson's dolphin	*Cephalorhynchus commersonii*
Harbor porpoise	*Phocoena phocoena*
Vaquita	*Phocoena sinus*
Burmeister's porpoise	*Phocoena spinipinnis*
Spectacled porpoise	*Phocoena dioptrica*
Dall's porpoise	*Phocoenoides dalli*
Finless porpoise	*Neophocaena phocaenoides*
Ganges susu	*Platanista gangetica*
Indus susu	*Platanista minor*
Boutu	*Inia geoffrensis*
Baiji	*Lipotes vexillifer*
Franciscana	*Pontoporia blainvillei*

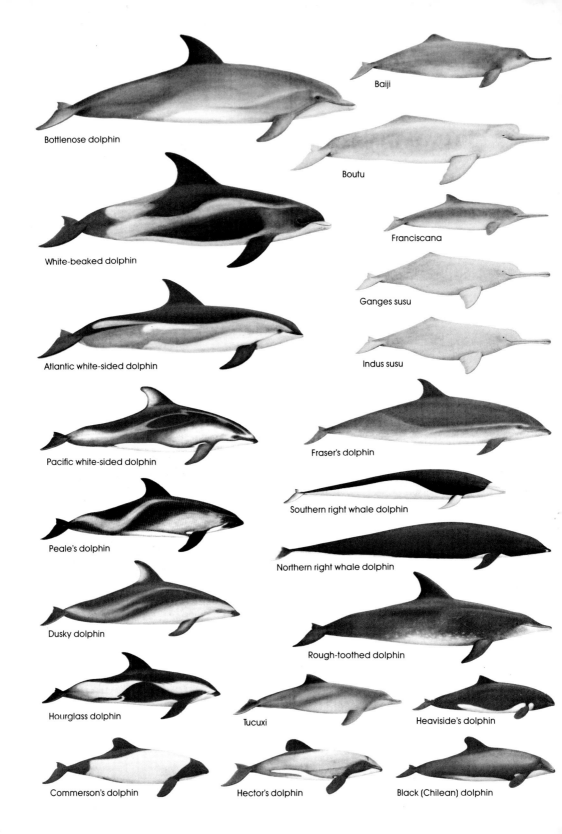

Bottlenose dolphin

Baiji

Boutu

White-beaked dolphin

Franciscana

Ganges susu

Atlantic white-sided dolphin

Indus susu

Pacific white-sided dolphin

Fraser's dolphin

Southern right whale dolphin

Peale's dolphin

Northern right whale dolphin

Dusky dolphin

Rough-toothed dolphin

Hourglass dolphin

Tucuxi

Heaviside's dolphin

Commerson's dolphin

Hector's dolphin

Black (Chilean) dolphin

mmon dolphin

Pan tropical spotted dolphin

o-Pacific humpbacked dolphin

Spinner dolphin

Atlantic humpbacked dolphin

Clymene dolphin

awaddy dolphin

Atlantic spotted dolphin

ess porpoise

Striped dolphin

porpoise

Pygmy killer whale

ectacled porpoise

Melon-headed whale

uita

Risso's dolphin

oor porpoise

eister's porpoise

A chart showing the names and relative sizes of thirty-nine
species of dolphins and porpoises.
Scale 1:42

SUGGESTIONS FOR FURTHER READING

Alpers, Antony. *Dolphins: The Myth and the Mammal.* Cambridge: The Riverside Press, 1961.

American Cetacean Society. *The Whalewatcher.* A quarterly journal with short articles on cetacean research and conservation. Published by the American Cetacean Society, P.O. Box 2639, San Pedro, California 90731.

Baker, Alan N. *Whales and Dolphins of New Zealand and Australia: An Identification Guide.* Wellington, N.Z.: Victoria Press, 1983.

Boschung, H. T., Jr., J. D. Williams, D. W. Gotshall, D. K. Caldwell, and M. C. Caldwell. *The Audubon Society Field Guide to North American Fishes, Whales, and Dolphins.* New York: Alfred A. Knopf, n.d.

Caldwell, David K. and Melba C. *The World of the Bottlenose Dolphin.* Philadelphia and New York: J. B. Lippincott, 1972.

Ellis, Richard. *Dolphins and Porpoises.* New York: Alfred A. Knopf, 1982.

Evans, William. "Orientation Behavior of Delphinids: Radiotelemetric Studies." *Annals New York Academy of Sciences,* Vol. 188, 1971, pp. 142–60.

Gaskin, D. E. *The Ecology of Whales and Dolphins.* London and Exeter, New Hampshire: Heinemann, 1982.

Haley, Delphine, ed. *Marine Mammals of Eastern North Pacific and Arctic Waters.* Second (revised) edition. Seattle: Pacific Search Press, 1986.

Herman, Louis M., ed. *Cetacean Behavior: Mechanisms and Functions.* New York: John Wiley & Sons, 1980.

Kanwisher, John W., and Sam H. Ridgway. "The Physiological Ecology of Whales and Porpoises." *Scientific American,* Vol. 248, No. 6 (June 1983) pp. 110–120.

Katona, Steven K., Valerie Rough, and David T. Richardson. *A Field Guide to the Whales, Porpoises and Seals of the Gulf of Maine and Eastern Canada: Cape Cod to Newfoundland.* New York: Charles Scribner's Sons, 1983.

Leatherwood, Stephen, David K. Caldwell, and Howard E. Winn. *Whales, Dolphins, and Porpoises of the Western North Atlantic: A Guide to Their Identification.* National Oceanic and Atmospheric Administration, National Marine Fisheries Service, NOAA Technical Report NMFS Circular 396, 1976.

Leatherwood, Stephen, Randall R. Reeves, William F. Perrin, and William E. Evans. *Whales, Dolphins, and Porpoises of the Eastern North Pacific and Adjacent Arctic Waters: A Guide to Their Identification.* National Oceanic and Atmospheric Administration, National Marine Fisheries Service, NOAA Technical Report NMFS Circular 444, 1982.

Leatherwood, Stephen, and Randall R. Reeves. *The Sierra Club Handbook of Whales and Dolphins.* San Francisco: Sierra Club Books, 1983.

Norris, Kenneth S. *The Porpoise Watcher.* New York: W. W. Norton, 1974.

Norris, Kenneth S., and Bertel Møhl. "Can Odontocetes Debilitate Prey with Sound?" *American Naturalist,* Vol. 122, 1983, pp. 85–104.

Pryor, Karen. *Lads Before the Wind: Adventures in Porpoise Training.* New York: Harper and Row, 1975.

Ridgway, Sam H. "Homeostasis in the Aquatic Environment." In *Mammals of the Sea: Biology and Medicine,* S. H. Ridgway, ed. Springfield, Illinois: Charles C Thomas, 1972, pp. 590–747.

Ridgway, Sam H., and Richard Harrison, eds. *Handbook of Marine Mammals.* Volumes 4 and 5. London: Academic Press, in press.

Winn, Howard E., and Bori L. Olla, eds. *Behavior of Marine Animals: Current Perspectives in Research.* Volume 3: *Cetaceans.* New York: Plenum Press, 1979.

Würsig, Bernd. "Dolphins." *Scientific American,* Vol. 240, No. 3 (March 1979), pp. 136–148.

Würsig, Bernd, and Melanie Würsig. "Day and Night of the Dolphin." *Natural History,* Vol. 88, No. 3 (March, 1979), pp. 60–67.

INDEX

Italicized page numbers refer to illustrations.

A

Age: methods of determining dolphins', 48
Amazon River, 36, 41
Amphibians, 18
Anchovies, 59–60, 99, 100
Antarctic Convergence, 75
Aquarial Gardens (Boston), 80
Aquariums, 80
Aristotle, 9
Atlantic humpbacked dolphins, 51
Atlantic white-sided dolphins, 58
Awbrey, Frank, 35

B

Baiji (dolphin), 36, *38*, 87, 102
Bats, 30, 32
Beluga (whale), 42, *78–79*
"Bends," 29–30
Biosonar. See Sonar
Birds: and dolphins, 60–61
Birth: of river dolphins, 39; of captive dolphins, 87–89
Black cod (fish), 100
Blood: and body temperature, 27
Blowhole, 21, *22*
Blubber, 24, 26, 54
Blue whales, 85
Body temperature (of dolphins): regulation of, 24–27
Bones (of dolphins), 81
Bottlenose dolphins: characteristics of, 33, *35*, *44–46*, 47–48, *49*, 51–*53*; transporting of, 80–82, 84; birth of captive, 87; as food, 99. See also "Tuffy"
Boutu (dolphin), *13*, 36–39, *40*, 41, 101–2
Brains (of dolphins), 32–33
Breathing, 11
Burmeister's porpoises, 55

C

Cetacea (order of), 10–11, 19–21, 30
Changjiang (river, China), 36, 38, 102
Chilean dolphins, 55
Clymene dolphins, 72

Coastal dolphins, 12, 44–57
Cochita. See Vaquita
Commerson's dolphins, *10*, 55–57, *78–79*, *81*, 82, *87*
Common dolphins, *14*, 63, *64*, 65–66
Communication: with dolphins, 33–35; between species, 39–41
Continental-shelf dolphins, 12, 14, 58–67
Counter-current heat-exchanger, 26–27

D

Dall's porpoises, 56, *57*, 97, 99
"Didi" (a spinner dolphin), 66
Diet: of boutu and tucuxi, 39; of bottlenose dolphins, 45, 47
Diving, 27–30
Dolphinarium, 80
Dolphins: evolution of, 18–23; and fish herding, 43; as people-helpers, 49–52; captive, 78–89; endangered, 87, 100–104; and competition with humans for food, 90–100; as food, 92–93, 99–100. See also Coastal dolphins; Continental-shelf dolphins; Oceanic dolphins; River dolphins; *Body parts; Characteristics; Specific species*
Domestication (of dolphins), 78–79
Dorado (fish), 11
Dorsal fin: lack of blubber on, 24, 26; scars on, 48; on Atlantic humpbacked dolphin, 52; on Risso's dolphin, 72; on rough-toothed dolphin, 73; on killer whale, 84
Duisburg Zoo, 87
Dusky dolphins, *20*, 58–59, *60*, *62*

E

Ears (of dolphins), 9, 30. See also Echolocation; Sounds
Echolocation, 9, 30–32, 41, 42
Elephant seals, 104
Endangered dolphins, 87, 100–104

F

Finless porpoises, *42*
Fish: contrasted with mammals, 10–11; herding of, 43; "whacking" of, 47. See also Anchovies; Mullet; Remora; Tuna fishing
Flexibility: of boutus, 41